Sermons For Pentecost I Based On First Lesson Texts For Cycle C

How Long Will You Limp?
(Because God Is Tired Of The Bull)

Carlyle Fielding Stewart, III

CSS Publishing Company, Inc., Lima, Ohio

SERMONS FOR PENTECOST I BASED ON FIRST LESSON TEXTS
FOR CYCLE C: HOW LONG WILL YOU LIMP?

Copyright © 1997 by
CSS Publishing Company, Inc.
Lima, Ohio

All rights reserved. No part of this publication may be reproduced in any manner whatsoever without the prior permission of the publisher, except in the case of brief quotations embodied in critical articles and reviews. Inquiries should be addressed to: Permissions, CSS Publishing Company, Inc., P.O. Box 4503, Lima, Ohio 45802-4503.

Scripture quotations are from the *New Revised Standard Version of the Bible*, copyright 1989 by the Division of Christian Education of the National Council of the Churches of Christ in the USA. Used by permission.

Library of Congress Cataloging-in-Publication Data

Stewart, Carlyle Fielding, 1951-
   Sermons for Pentecost I based on first lesson texts for cycle C : how long will you limp? because God is tired of the bull / Carlyle Fielding Stewart, III.
     p. cm.
   ISBN 0-7880-1050-6 (pbk.)
   1. Pentecost season—Sermons. 2. Bible. O.T.—Sermons. 3. Sermons, American. I. Title.
BV4300.5.S74   1997
252'.64—dc21
                                                      96-46505
                                                        CIP

This book is available in the following formats, listed by ISBN:
   0-7880-1050-6 Book
   0-7880-1051-4 Mac
   0-7880-1052-2 IBM 3 1/2
   0-7880-1077-8 Sermon Prep

PRINTED IN U.S.A.

*For those
who
preach*

and

*To the memory of
Rev. Dr. Henry Elijah Stewart
Rev. Dr. Carlyle Fielding Stewart, Sr.*

Editor's Note Regarding The Lectionary

During the past two decades there has been an attempt to move in the direction of a uniform lectionary among various Protestant denominations.

Preaching on the same scripture lessons every Sunday is a step in the right direction of uniting Christians of many faiths. If we are reading the same scriptures together, we may also begin to accomplish other achievements. Our efforts will be strengthened through our unity.

Beginning with Advent 1995 The Evangelical Lutheran Church in America dropped its own lectionary schedule and adopted the Revised Common Lectionary.

Reflecting this change, resources published by CSS Publishing Company put their major emphasis on the Revised Common Lectionary texts for the church year.

Table Of Contents

Preface   7

Pentecost   9
    The Spirit Of Pentecost
    Acts 2:1-21

The Holy Trinity   17
    When Wisdom Cries Out
    Proverbs 8:1-4, 22-31

Proper 4   25
Pentecost 2
Ordinary Time 9
    How Long Will You Limp?
    (Because God Is Tired Of The Bull)
    1 Kings 18:20-39

Corpus Christi   33
    They Didn't Have To Do It, But They Did
    Genesis 14:18-20

Proper 5   39
Pentecost 3
Ordinary Time 10
    In Times Of Need
    1 Kings 17:8-24

Proper 6   45
Pentecost 4
Ordinary Time 11
    Extreme Measures
    1 Kings 21:1-21a

Proper 7   51
Pentecost 5
Ordinary Time 12
    Nowhere To Run, Nowhere To Hide
    1 Kings 19:1-15a

Proper 8   59
Pentecost 6
Ordinary Time 13
    A Double Dose
    2 Kings 2:1-2, 6-14

Proper 9   67
Pentecost 7
Ordinary Time 14
    What Money Can't Buy
    2 Kings 5:1-14

Proper 10   73
Pentecost 8
Ordinary Time 15
    A Tale Of Two "Cities"
    Amos 7:1-17

Lectionary Preaching After Pentecost   81

Preface

In wrestling with a title for this book, I kept thinking about how cumbersome it must have been for Elijah to enter a contest whose centerpiece was bull sacrifice. The prophets of Baal were certain what their gods would do with their bulls and Elijah was confident that the bull he offered for sacrifice would be consumed by God's fires, thus revealing the superiority of his God over the gods of Baal.

However, in thinking more about this, a deeper truth about bull sacrifice became evident to me and that is how easily the people of God are so beset with the ritual and routine of sacrifice that they often forget its original significance and intent. So instead of sac-rifice clarifying for the people of God the means of atonement and providing ways of attaining a deeper spirituality, they incur spiritual ambivalence, which causes them to waver or limp between the ambiguity of what God has promised to do and the surety that God will make good on the promise. Apart from the traditional inter-pretations of the meaning of bulls and sacrifice, a deeper concern is the manner in which the ritual of ceremonial sacrifices makes routine our spiritual certainty about what God truly expects of us.

These realities signify the parentheses of our spiritual striving. Elijah asks the fundamental question, "How long will you limp between two opinions?" I believe that this question raises a dilemma in which we Christians often find ourselves. Sometimes we limp between doubt and certainty, between clarity and confusion, between an unequivocal affirmation of faith and a lingering hesitation of God's promises to God's people.

Accordingly, we have offered God our sacrifices for atonement and still we are unclear that God will cleanse, forgive, and finally renew us. The prophetic task is to cut through the machinations, doubts, and deception created by spiritual ambiguity. The experiences of Elijah, Elisha, and Amos shared in this book of sermons are lessons for the people of God and the church today.

In this age of drug addiction, violence, family disintegration, and spiritual apostasy and disaffection, the church must raise a prophetic voice amid these concerns, which means calling the people back to God and challenging the existing order to transform itself so as to realize and build the kingdom of God. This means that the leaders of the nations and the people of God must stand with firm conviction and certainty that God is not a liar and that those who try to follow God and practice the central tenets of the faith will finally be neither abandoned nor disillusioned.

The prophets provide a lesson in courage by not looking the other way in the face of evil and not allowing those forces of evil to intimidate the people of God and corrupt God's will. They also teach us the value of claiming our convictions and believing absolutely that the God of Abraham, Isaac and Jacob, the God of Israel, that Christ does not waver in his love of us.

We can learn much from the prophets because it is their holy boldness, their willingness to stand against the powers and principalities that enables us to cut through the spiritual ambiguities of our age. The prophetic voice speaks with resonance and clarity amid the dissonance and discord of our times.

It is my hope that these sermons illuminate the passion, courage, and resolve of those prophets who stood for love, truth, and justice and sacrificed their own lives so that spiritual uncertainty could be forever vanquished as we seek to know God. We must do more than offer our bulls of sacrifice. We must be willing to speak the truth in these troubled times to a dying world and claim our faith as a firm foundation of God's promises for the future.

The Spirit Of Pentecost

Pentecost   ***Acts 2:1-21***

It was one of the most wonderful and exciting moments in the history of the Christian faith. The Holy Spirit had fallen fresh on the lives of believers. People were filled with the passion and fires of the Holy Ghost. They were shouting joy from all directions. They were gathered from every persuasion and city, every nation and province, all glorifying God, speaking in foreign tongues but understanding each other, expressing different voices but still in one accord. This was the time of Pentecost, when God saw fit to pour out the spirit which spawned the birth of the Christian Church.

Today we need the fervor, fire, tongues, passion, and Spirit of Pentecost. Today the Christian Church needs a rebirth of the spirit, where souls are on fire with the love of Christ, where barriers are broken down and superficial divisions which sequester and divide people are bridged through a unity of the Spirit. Today more than ever the church needs to recapture the fires of Pentecost so that souls can break free from bondage, and healing, deliverance, and the full power of God's anointing can be experienced in every medium and every idiom by people filled with Holy Ghost madness.

Too many churches today are devoid of the Spirit of Pentecost because they are dry, stale, and discordant, where parishioners are in a somnambulist stupor; where worship services are vapid, staid, and wooden; where the preaching is dull, flat, and insipid; where the singing is Geritol-tired and without the vim, verve, and verse which speaks of a crucified, died and risen Lord; where if anyone taps his foot and says, "Amen," he is stared into silence, and if anyone shouts, "Thank you, Jesus," or "Help me, Holy Ghost," parishioners call EMS, the DS or 911! Too many churches have become mausoleums for the dead rather than coliseums of praise for a living God. They have lost the spirit of Pentecost! They have lost their enthusiasm. They have lost their joy for Jesus and find themselves suffering from what William Willimon calls "Institutional and Spiritual Dry Rot." Pentecost marks the beginning of a new spiritual movement in Christ; a movement birthed through the fires of the Holy Spirit; a movement steeped in the spirit of hope, renewal, and spiritual transformation. It is a movement where souls are on fire with the passion of the Holy Spirit and the Church today more than ever needs to recapture that spirit. If the Church is to survive the next millennium it must recapture some of the praise and enthusiasm it had two millennia ago. The spiritual energy and vitality of Pentecost has sustained the Church through two millennia.

What then is this Pentecostal Spirit?

First, it is the spirit of a people fully open to the anointive outpouring of the Holy Spirit! One writer said the Christian religion can be divided into two basic groups: those who have been trained to constrain or hold the Spirit within and those open to expressing or letting go of the Spirit!

In the first group, the discipline of self-control must be practiced at all times, where the believer will not lose control of himself in the Spirit because it is intellectually, ethically, and behaviorally inappropriate. Religion in this instance culminates in the believer's capacity to be still and listen, to be silent and contemplative in the things of the Spirit. To express oneself openly is synonymous with losing control of oneself. The point here is never to become too emotional, passionate, or outwardly expressive of the movement of the Holy Spirit upon and within one's life. The thing here is always to maintain control and not allow the Spirit to have too much latitude and freedom. The Spirit in this group expresses itself primarily in cognitive, contemplative modalities. The virtues of religious expression reach their zenith in the things of the mind which reflect self-control, discipline, and restraint and encourage a disciplined and passionately restrained demonstration of faith.

The second group are those entreating the Spirit to come in and have its way, which always culminates in the outward, emotional, enthusiastic expression of religious faith and belief. The point is not to maintain control cognitively but to allow the Spirit to come in to express itself through the person. The goal here is for each believer to clear oneself of all external restraints and worries so that the Holy Spirit may come in, take up residency in the human soul, and transport the believer into higher realms of spiritual consciousness and expression. This is achieved by opening the door to the Spirit and permitting it to come in and use the person to reach a previously unrealized domain of spiritual consciousness.

So in the first group, the Spirit is controlled by the person's capacity to reach a certain level of restrained disciplinary expression. In the second group, the Spirit freely takes believers to heights of mind, body, spirit and soul previously unattained.

I believe the Spirit of Pentecost was reflected in a third group, which was a combination of these two. The people had a profoundly life-changing cognitive experience with the Holy Spirit, but it was so deep and cataclysmic that it transported them into new and higher realms of consciousness and religious expression. I believe that these cognitive and emotive groups, one which is primarily internal and contemplative in religious expression and the other more external and passionate, created and reached the third tier of religious expression at Pentecost that culminated in an explosion of the Spirit and the realization of a whole new level of spiritual belief and understanding among them.

First, what made Pentecost so deep and life transforming was that perhaps for the first time in human history these two modalities of religious expression, the cognitive and the emotive, one internal and contemplative, the other external and expressive, reached a spiritual synthesis. For the first time in human history these two separate groups became one group, filled with the Holy Ghost, reaching previously unrealized heights in thought, spirit, mind, body, and soul never before reached by human beings in the history of humankind. These two groups became one group which reached a third realm of religious belief, passion, and expression because they were all open to the outpouring and anointing of the Holy Spirit. Whatever intellectual or emotional barriers separated and kept them divided were demolished because they were all receptive to the full outpouring of the Holy Spirit. This means the intellectuals were cognitively filled by and fulfilled in the Holy Spirit. This means those more emotionally and passionately expressive of their faith were filled by and fulfilled in the Holy Spirit to the point that there were no distinctions between them and they all became one. It was because of the Spirit's anointing and because they were open to the Spirit of outpouring upon them that they were all able to glorify God.

This is the power of the Spirit's anointing. Anointing is derived from the Greek verb *Chrio* which means "anointing or oil of gladness" which corresponds with the Greek noun *Chrisma* which is "a pouring out, upon, or into from without." This is one meaning of the word "anointing." It is something that moves from without to within and from within to without. It is something conferred by God through the movement of the Holy Spirit. This Chrisma's outpouring enabled these various groups to reach new power and heights in spiritual consciousness and belief, but it was because of their openness to the Spirit's anointing and outpouring that the Spirit of Pentecost was achieved.

What we need is the spirit of openness and receptiveness to the Spirit's outpouring; to the promise and capacity of the Holy Spirit to transport, translate, and transcend us to higher heights in our faith, belief and the contemplation and expression of that faith. The more we are open to the Spirit's outpouring, the more we lose personal control and give control to the Holy Spirit, the greater is our knowledge, power, and ability to express and interpret matters of the Spirit.

Second, the Spirit of Pentecost effected unity amid diversity by creating a common language of faith and belief. Although the believers were from many nations with different tongues, the Holy Spirit united them into one body of believers by forging a common language of faith and belief. With so much fire, power, and enthusiasm did the people speak that observers thought they were drunk on wine. The tongues of fire rested over each of them as they spoke in their various languages. Fire represents the Holy Spirit and purification.

Now the power of Pentecost was realized not only in the fact that people from different nations and language groups could all express themselves differently and be understood in unison by the sheer power of the Holy Spirit, but also by the capacity of the Holy Spirit to unify them when they spoke different languages spiritually.

What unifies a people nationally? The national language! What unifies the people spiritually? A common language of faith and belief from which they derive meaning, power, and purpose. Language has the power to unify consciousness, and thus the individual, into a single framework for interpretation.

In speaking the same language, we always presuppose the use of the same morphology, which is the structure of language; the same phonology, which is the sound of language; the same vocabulary; the same syntax, which are rules for arranging words; and the same lexicon, which is the total stock of words in a language. However, the connotation and denotation of words may be strangely different. One would assume that in speaking the same language we all have the same meaning.

Similarly, we may all draw from the same spiritual lexicon but arrive at different meanings in the practice of spirituality which lead to confusion and division among us. Spiritually speaking, we may all draw from the same morphology, phonology, vocabulary, syntax, and lexicon of Christian belief, but may not have the unity and power of the Holy Spirit to place us in one accord. These variations are just as present in the *content* of spirituality as the *mode* and *style* by which the content of belief is expressed and conveyed.

What do we mean here? People may speak different national languages and dialects which make communication with foreigners unintelligible, but they can also speak different languages of faith and spirituality which keep them divided as a faith community.

Because we speak the same language does not mean we understand the full depths and breadths of its meaning. The same is true in the Church. Because we speak a common language about Christ does not mean we experience a common faith and understanding in Christ!

On a deeper level, the Spirit of Pentecost united people so that those speaking different languages of faith and spiritual belief could move toward spiritual consensus and unity, for there is power in unity. Accordingly, in many ways the divisions of spiritual language, of faith and spiritual belief, do more to separate and divide people than anything else. What keeps good Christians confused and polarized? The inability to come to terms with those divisions regarding basic hermeneutics, that is to say, what is interpreted, why it is interpreted, and how it is interpreted.

The Spirit of Pentecost unified people not only across national language barriers but also across barriers of spiritual meaning and consciousness which had prevented their unity as one spiritual people. God knew that the spiritual language barriers do more to keep people apart than the natural language barriers. Sometimes people who cannot speak the same language will find ways to communicate. Sometimes it is through sign language or facial expressions or by using words which sound similar in the other's language. Whatever the case, they find a common ground which allows them to communicate meaning fully. This is the Spirit of Pentecost!

In reviewing your Bibles and studying the early Church, the work of the apostles and others, you will find numerous divisions regarding spiritual belief and practice. Paul speaks to it in Corinthians regarding the matter of spiritual gifts and speaking in tongues. He discusses conflict around circumcision and other matters of the faith. Paul speaks to the issues of divisions among the people, which were primarily spiritual, doctrinal, and behavioral. Even after Pentecost, the people were separated on the nature and practice of Christian belief.

So the power of Pentecost culminated in the realization that those divisions did not ultimately matter. What mattered was unity of the Spirit where all believers were in one accord for Christ!

This meant they could still be one people notwithstanding their differences!

This is interesting, because you can have people in the same church, in the same denomination, speaking different spiritual languages almost to the point of unintelligibility. This can be a problem also with a church where you have so many people from different denominational traditions. This is good, but much confusion and strife ensue about how things are done. This can be a source of consternation and further polarization among believers through the blessings of the Holy Spirit.

The Spirit of Pentecost as the unifying language of the Holy Spirit helps people to get in one accord. Where the superficial barriers which divide, polarize, and ultimately alienate people are overcome because believers have been opened to the Spirit's anointive outpouring power, they thereby overcome the divisions which keep them fragmented.

The Spirit of Pentecost is the Spirit of unity, of realizing the things we have in common through a unified language of faith and belief. Such language recognizes the right to be different but ultimately unifies people into one body of believers through the blessings of the Holy Spirit.

This is why there was so much power, because they all spoke in the language of the Holy Spirit which effects unity, power, purpose, and single-mindedness amid diversity.

Third, the Spirit of Pentecost was actualized in the collective realization of the power of the Holy Spirit. The Spirit not only was poured out and also raised people beyond their divisions, but the Spirit did it collectively. Can you realize what power and joy are in store when believers come to consensus in the spirit and realize it collectively? What made Pentecost such a powerful experience is that the Holy Spirit was poured out on a mass aggregate: a congregation, a collective of people, and not just individually. This means that the whole body of believers were immersed in the energy and power of the Spirit. Can you conceive of such power when true believers come together in one accord for Christ? Can you imagine the walls that are knocked down, the divisions that are mended, the strife and impediments overcome for the Glory of God? Can you imagine the joy God the Father, the Son and the Holy Ghost had at such a willing display of humility and obedience to the things of God? Can you imagine how winds swept and the earth shook with gladness and joy because finally the people came together of one mind and one spirit?

This is exactly what is needed today: the spirit of outpouring and anointing; the spirit of people speaking in tongues of fire as a united entity for Christ; the spirit of consensus; the spirit of joy, hope, and power; the spirit of love and heightened expectations of what God can do through the people of God; the spirit of reconciliation; the spirit of transcendence, transportation, and deliverance; the spirit of the power of the Holy Spirit!

This is the spirit which gave birth to the Church. This spirit is the power of Pentecost! It is a redeeming, sanctifying, and liberating experience which compels the people of God to reduce the things we have in difference rather than the things we have in common. This is the Spirit of Pentecost: a spirit needed in our churches and the world today! Amen!

When Wisdom Cries Out

The Holy Trinity *Proverbs 8:1-4, 22-31*

This text of Proverbs, attributed to Solomon but most probably written by sages, teachers, and bureaucrats of the intellectual elite of Israel and Judah, reflects an urgent cry for wisdom throughout the land. The people are in need of wisdom, and wisdom is in search of people who will practice its virtues and extol forever the higher principles of courage, justice, righteousness, and truth. The absence of wisdom is folly. The beginning of wisdom is the fear and respect of God.

Where then is wisdom? Where then is knowledge of God? Where then are people who embody and espouse its higher values and who are the sacred keepers of her holy writ? It is no accident that the writer uses the imagery of woman's wisdom as a means of personifying the exigency and urgency of the need for wisdom throughout the nation. Will anyone hear? Does anyone understand the need for knowledge and truth anymore? Have the values and principles which ensured and consolidated our strength as a nation and people withered on the vines of frivolity, depravity, and indifference? Even wisdom itself cries out in utter consternation!

It is no accident that the writer here uses a kind of literary irony, antiphrasis, and satire to dramatize the point of the need for wisdom to find a place in the human mind and heart. Since the people will not seek wisdom, wisdom then, paradoxically, must seek refuge in the minds, hearts, and souls of true seekers and believers. Since the people have virtually ceased their search for those deeper things of God, life and creation, wisdom must leave its portals, abandon its gates, and relinquish its sacred shrines, safe houses, and sacred texts to search for true takers and seekers. Wisdom thus has enough savvy to seek new venues among the people even when the people don't strive to seek and attain it.

In reading this passage we might say that many of the same problems and distractions facing the people of Israel and ancient societies still plague us today. Wisdom is crying out more than ever before: crying out for souls who will seek, embody, and practice her precepts so that the people will return to a true knowledge and love of God. Then people of God and the larger society shall realize righteousness, wholeness, and peace. Where then do we see it crying out?

Wisdom is crying out for peace in the streets of this land. Fear stalks, terrorizes, and imprisons us. Some communities and neighborhoods are under siege. Gone are the days when you could leave your house unlocked and go to the corner store to return and find everything intact. Gone are the days when you could take a leisurely stroll without worrying about someone knocking you over the head. In this day of drive-by shootings, and explosions and implosions in buildings and airplanes, where innocent people die painful and senseless deaths, in these times of knife-brandishing, gun-toting street mercenaries who take the lives of people over a dollar and some change, wisdom is crying out for sanity and light. Wisdom is crying out for peace and the cessation of wholesale, unmitigated violence in the streets.

One man still grieves the loss of his father, who, on one of his daily strolls in a rural Southern community, was accosted by several boys and beaten to death with a tire iron because he had no money with which they could buy crack cocaine.

An elderly woman, who had been missing several days, was found dead in her home. Her throat was slit and her money missing. Three teenagers were later caught and charged with murder. They were thirteen, fifteen, and sixteen years old. Wisdom cries out for law and order. Wisdom cries out for sanity amid the demonic and insane forces of society. Wisdom cries out for a reverence for life amid desacralizing and desecrating forces of evil in the land.

Our streets are filled with litanies of pain and grief, where internecine strife undermines our sense of trust and belonging. Insecurity anywhere is a threat to security everywhere. **Wisdom cries out for peace and the eradication of senseless, demented violence in the streets of the land.**

Wisdom is crying out for love in the families of this land. The term "family values" has received much ridicule since the statement of Dan Quayle, but the truth is, nothing is needed more today than the practice of those beliefs and values which make strong, viable families. The disintegration of every society in some form or another can be ascribed to the dissolution of the family. As the primary social unit, the family provides cohesion, stability, and training for its members. There is an adage which says, "If we love our children in the high chair, we won't see them in the electric chair."

Many people recall the days when families sat around the radio or the television set, shared nightly meals together, and discussed family business. Parents monitored the television viewing of their children partly because there was only one set but also because the programs contained not nearly the violence we see today. There seemed to be a sense of togetherness, where families looked out for other families, where serious family discussions occurred about matters of ultimate and serious concern. Opportunities for sharing created occasions for dialogue, learning, and the reinforcement of positive values among family members.

Today, many homes have a television set in every room and family meals are seldom, if ever, shared. Parents don't take time to talk with their children to educate them and be educated by them. Parents appear oblivious to what's troubling their children. Wisdom cries out for genuine dialogue and quality time as families are like ships passing in the night. One writer said the greatest inheritance we can give our children is a little time each day.

My father related the story about how his father cautioned him about hanging with the wrong crowd, but he kept ignoring his father's advice. One day his father called him into his room to pray about the matter with his son. "Now I don't want you running with these boys again," exhorted the father. "But, Dad," said the boy, "I'm not better than they are." "I'm not saying you are better than they are," said the father. "I'm saying that you have a better opportunity to make something out of your life." This young man never forgot this lesson and that his father would often take the time to impart such wisdom. Moreover, prayer was an important element in family life. The family took time to pray and to ask God's guidance in all things.

Wisdom cries out for families to teach each other and to pray for one another. One recent study said approximately ninety percent of Christians never have family prayer or Bible study. They are too busily preoccupied with other things to pray. They are too distracted with the world, too saturated with "getting and spending," in the words of the poet Wordsworth. As the teenage daughter of a parishioner once quipped, "Why do we have to pray? God takes too long to answer anyway!" In this world of the mad dash and the quick hash, people too readily expect the quick fix and immediate results in the challenges they are facing. Theirs is a slot machine faith. Put the coin in the first time and hit the big payday! But God is still God. God is still in charge of all things. A great tragedy today is not simply disobeying God, but living as though God did not exist.

Unfortunately, this girl was not taught that there is power in prayer, that God answers in God's own time. She couldn't fathom that just a little time in prayer might make things all right and just a little talk with Jesus will help things turn out right. Wisdom cries out for more families to have prayer and devotional time, time for caring, sharing, and genuine listening and interaction. If more families did this, perhaps we wouldn't have the level of destruction, disintegration, and disaffection we see among various youths and adults today. **Wisdom cries out for prayer, caring, sharing, teaching, and learning within the family circle.**

Wisdom is crying out for morals and ethics in the culture of this land. In a culture of commercialization and exploitation, the fast buck is God. One writer said that if we took the words, "In God We Trust," from our currency, we could replace them with the words, "We Need Thee Every Hour." In a society where sex and violence are glorified for profits, we don't grasp the wisdom of how such things adversely affect the values of our children!

In music and videos, violence, sex, and foul language are highly touted because they increase the profits. Many videos have these codes: V for violence, N for nudity, AL for adult language, and AC for adult content. Some music contains warning labels about explicit lyrics and categorizes the content as "cussing" or "non-cussing." In a society where anything which increases profits is marketed, commercialized, and exploited, wisdom cries out for the prophet, the truth teller, the warrior who will have the courage to tell it like it is. Not *profits,* but *prophets* are needed today. People who will speak the truth and call the culture and society into account for the shameless culture of exploitation and the dissemination of anything that will sell, particularly when what is sold destroys the capacity of our children to discern what is just, moral, and righteous.

Reinhold Niebuhr in his *Christ and Culture* reminds us of the following: "The most vicious thing, of course, is social, pagan religion, with its polytheism and idolatry, its beliefs and rites, its sensuality and commercialization. Such religion, however, is interfused with ... other institutions of society so that the Christian is in constant danger of compromising his loyalty to the Lord" (p. 453).

Wisdom cries out for boldness and courage, for the discerning, daring, and undashed to stand before the powers and principalities and espouse the truth of the exploitative and denigrating aspects of American culture. Must everything be sold? Are there no limits to what the larger culture can propagate for profit?

Wisdom is crying out for caring in the schools of this land. Many recent reports have lamented the declining state of public education, where the illiteracy and dropout rates are escalating enormously, where teachers are so beset with disciplinary problems with some students that they can't teach the other students. The problems of crime and violence in schools are cause for much concern.

Where is the wisdom of administrators and educators, parents and others in combating the problems of education? While more funding is helpful, more commitment on the part of parents and others is needed to provide children with an education which will allow them to compete in tomorrow's world. Parents then must view schools as more than drop-off places and teachers as more than glorified baby-sitters. But where is the wisdom? Where is the relentless and tireless search for answers to fix the problem? One teacher remarked that she is so fed up now that all she does is come to work, collect her paycheck, and go home! The problem is our educated elite, the teachers who teach and administrators who lead, are at a loss to resolve the current crises. Direct linkages exist between illiteracy, violence, and other social maladies. Wisdom is crying out for solutions which will effect positive results. If the schools die, the people will perish! **Wisdom is crying out for positive change and transformation in the schools throughout this land.**

Finally, wisdom is crying out for courage in the churches and religious institutions of the land. Thankfully, many people are returning to church. Regrettably, the Church too often has remained a nameless, silent accomplice in the duplicities and calamities of society. Church and state should work together, but the Church cannot shirk its responsibility in rebuking and reproving the ills of the social order. Moreover, the Church should do more than criticize, but must equally energize the masses to confront the problems and effect positive solutions. Where is the Church in addressing the various troubles which plague us? Where is the Church in eradicating poverty and oppression, disaffection and depression in the land?

The writers of Proverbs understood that a return to wisdom inherently meant a return to God and those things sacred. The Church must return to the wisdom of God if the larger society is to retrieve a sense of cohesion and unity. The problem is the exilic consciousness of the church; a consciousness which has insulated itself against the harsher realities of evil; a consciousness which has established its own comfort zones by isolating itself from its vital sources and extant truths, from a God of the Exodus, a God of salvation, and a God of liberation.

Wisdom cries out in the churches and religious institutions of the land for a return to the seminal sources of spiritual vitality, which energize the church in its fight against evil and injustice. Helmut Thielicke warns against having our "proclamatory power" domesticated and sunk into a customary piety. Wisdom cries out for the people of God to vault those spiritual inanities and ecclesiastical insanities which bind and suppress our verse and verve and which transmute our concern for truth and wisdom into liturgical quagmires of mediocrity and silence.

If wisdom cries out anywhere, it cries out in the church, in the practice of spirituality, in the undaunted explication of pure, unsullied truth, in the need for religious and spiritual leaders to break free from the spell of fear and apathy cast upon them by society and culture like the shadows of Babylon.

Needed today is a theology of wisdom and truth, rooted in the wisdom and truth of Christ, which embraces but transcends the ephemeral, fluctuating truths of the marketplace and imparts its own archives of value and meaning, unfettered by the constraints and exploits of culture.

Wisdom cries out throughout the land. Are there no takers? No takers for the deeper insights, the studied and ponderous reflections which have quickened our resolve and tempered our steps? No takers for knowledge and prescience which illuminate the light of God on our darkened paths? Where are the seekers of wisdom in the streets, at the city gates, in our homes, in our culture, in our schools, and in our neighborhoods? Where are the seekers of love and light and truth in society and in the church? Truth tellers, where are you? Torchbearers, where are you? Flame showers where are you? Seed growers, where are you? Men, women, and children of God, where are you? Teachers, preachers and reachers, prophets, sages and crossbearers, where are you? Wisdom cries out!

Let us stop her crying by being more inquisitive, courageous, caring, and committed. Let us stop her crying by being *prophetic* rather than *profitic*. Let us pray, teach, and reach more to those in need. Let us stand boldly, undauntedly, for love, truth, and justice throughout the land. Let us cease her crying so she may find her place in every heart and every home, in every mind and in every dome where the spirit of knowledge, truth and God exists. How long shall wisdom cry before we respond to her cries? Amen!

How Long Will You Limp?
(Because God Is Tired of The Bull)

Proper 4   **1 Kings 18:20-39**
Pentecost 2
Ordinary Time 9

Elijah's magnificent display of strength and courage in facing and challenging the prophets of Baal is instructive for us. He has staked his ground on the summit of Carmel, located in Western Israel at the entrance of the Jezreel Valley. He has braced himself for the fallout. He has taken a firm stand without compunctions or remorse. He knows the wrath of Ahab and Jezebel shall soon be upon him. He knows the God he serves. He has tapped the power source of his faith. He is intrepid, undaunted, and undissolved in his determination to show forth the power and fires of his God. God is on his side. He is with God. See him now standing tall against the backdrop of green mountain terrain, a red sun, and blue sky.

The prophets of Baal have assembled. They are ready to meet the challenge. They will put forth their bull and see whose God is mightiest.

In this showdown Elijah poses the question of all questions which is the basis of the sermon today. This question forms the brackets, the parentheses, the two extremities of our striving for conviction and faith, for a relationship with God that is unwavering in the throes of life's battles. " 'How long will you go limping with two different opinions? If the Lord is God, follow him; but if Baal, then follow him.' The people did not answer him a word" (1 Kings 18:21).

This question forms the broader contours of our crucible of faith. How long shall we limp with two opinions? How long shall we waver between what God is and what Baal is? How long shall we ride the crests of doubt and uncertainty, playing mind games and Russian roulette in the things of God?

Elijah asks the question because he knows there remains lingering doubt among the people about God's power and majesty. He knows their volatility and vulnerability. He knows they still limp, that they have not yet made up their minds because they are confused about which God is which. He knows the people cannot yet walk with the brisk, unfaltering stride of absolute faith and confidence in the God of Israel. Like Jacob, their stride has been broken. They are limping on the plains of despair, doubt, and uncertainty. They are bemused and confused by the god of Baal; the god of fertility and storm; a god of the winds, fires, and rains; a god of the natural, cosmic elements. Unlike Jacob, their limp is a symbol of doubt rather than the mark of a new identity.

They have forgotten the God of Israel who has directed their paths; a God with whom they have forged a personal relationship; a God of the Exodus and the Jordan; a God who brought them into a new deal in a new land; a God who brought them through the desert, quarried waters from a rock, and set rainbows and clouds in arid desert oases. The people have forgotten about that God who brought them through, who kept them from annihilation by their enemies and vouched their safe passage through many dangers, toils, and snares. How quickly the people forget!

But is this not precisely the point? Does not a time come when we must absolutely, unequivocally, choose between the two opinions, where we can no longer vacillate on the thin lines of doubt and absolute conviction? A time when we must choose, aye or nay, between I will or I will not, where we must stand for something or fall for something? It is precisely the fluctuation which creates uncertainty. Somewhere and someplace we must take a stand, tall and firm, and have absolute faith and belief in

God and meet the challenges before us. Presenting the bull as a token of sacrifice is not enough. Wavering between two opinions will not suffice. A time comes when the bull is not enough. We must move beyond the bulls of sacrifice to full conviction and belief that God is able to make good on the promises! We must do more than present our bulls before God.

What then are these two opinions of which Elijah spoke which are equally the source of our bane and our blessing in our current context?

First is the God of Possibility versus the God of Disability. Elijah understood that God had helped the people through many challenges and difficulties in Israel, but God was invariably conceived as a God of possibility and not disability. The challenge for Israel as for the people of God today is to see God as the resource for overcoming deficits and disabilities as opposed to being a God who creates obstacles and barriers to wholeness and spirituality. God gives the people the capacity to overcome the hardships and trials of their lives. The ability to surmount the difficulties is often directly related to the power of belief and to cultivating a close, personal and meaningful relationship with God undergirded by a surety of conviction, and affirms absolute knowledge that God is God and that God is able to do all things. The God of Israel specialized in helping the people to overcome their deficits by enabling them to come into greater realization of themselves and God. The first theological premise for the God of Israel is an unyielding, unconditional belief that God is a God of possibility who enables people to overcome their disabilities along life's way.

Conversely, we have the gods of Baal who related to the people in terms of their disabilities. God is invariably conceived in terms of the disabilities and conditions created which foster disabling co-dependencies. God is always invoked in relation to personal weaknesses and not to strengths, and that is why the priests of Baal began slashing their wrists and engaging in self-denigration when their gods did not answer them after Elijah issued the challenge. It is true that Baal was conceived as the god of the storms who possessed magnificent strength, but that strength was never translated to the people in terms of their self-understanding of what their god could do through them instead of for them. Thus theologically speaking, the priests of Baal never conceived of their gods in terms of *their personal* power and strength, and what *they* could achieve through faith and trust in Baal.

We must remember that the basis of this challenge by Elijah was a raging drought in the land. Elijah's demonstration of God's power through fire was a reaffirmation of God's ability to show forth God's capacity to resolve a problem and God's ability to use God's people as instruments of God's creative possibilities. Because the priests of Baal had embraced a god who specialized in creating disabilities among the people, the prophet of Israel would prove that his God was just the opposite. How long will you limp between two opinions? Because God is tired of the bull.

As people of God today we cannot waver between a God of possibility and disability. We must have a positive faith in the power of God to make good on God's promises. This is the cornerstone of our faith and belief. The God we serve is one of raised expectations, high hopes and enormous possibilities.

Second is the God of Appeasement versus the God of Atonement. The priests of Baal presented their bull as a means of appeasing their God in order to evoke a specific response and to prove a point. Israel presented bulls to please and not to appease God, but also to atone for sins, as a genuine sacrifice to God. The bull presented to God by Elijah was substantive. It had deep personal meaning for the people. This was not a circus where people simply offered their sacrifices as a show of what God could do. Although it was a challenge to the priests of Baal, the act itself had deep spiritual meaning. The aim here was to please God and not to appease God.

Appeasing God means coaxing God to answer on our terms. The sacrifice therefore is not sincere. It is not offered from humble, contrite, and penitent hearts. It is done for show, to bribe God so we can obtain what we want. Pleasing God is accepting what God gives on God's terms and not using the sacrifice as a form of manipulation and machination. Pleasing God means offering the sacrifice as genuine means of atoning for our sins of omission and commission.

There once was a man who had a terrible car accident and recuperated in the hospital for five months with a broken back, a fractured skull, and two broken legs. All during his stay he promised God that if God made him well he would go to church and become a faithful Christian. His prayers amounted to appeasing and bribing God. The man never set foot inside a church after his convalescence. While in the hospital he thought if he appeased God, God would let him walk again. Fortunately for him, God blessed him despite his insincerity. He went back to his old ways without the thought of ever pleasing God.

Appeasing God is all form and no substance. Pleasing God is both form and substance, doing what is righteous and good in God's eyes. God may then respond on God's terms to the desires of our hearts.

Elijah understood as a prophet of God he must do what was pleasing to God. The bull he presented was consumed by fire, which at least gave the people bull burgers because it was offered as atonement, while the bull of the priests remained what it was, just bull, because it was offered as an appeasement. It was insincere and had no substance. How long shall you limp between the two opinions, because God is really tired of the bull!

God is tired of the bull of wavering, the bull of form without substance, the bull of show without sincerity, the bull of appeasement without atonement. A time comes when we must say what we mean and mean what we say, where we stand on conviction, trust that God is God, and do what God requires of us as the people of God!

The priests of Baal were in a dilemma. They were in an openly precarious situation. Elijah knew that talk was cheap and now it was time to put up or shut up. Some knew that their god simply did not respond on such terms. They knew that their bull would not meet the test, but they had no choice. They had to go along with the demonstration, so they gathered in a crowd, thinking that they could make up in numbers what they didn't have in faith. Elijah was one man who stood on the strength of conviction and his firm belief in God. This was no play thing. He was serious about making his point about which God was more resourceful and responsive to the needs of the people!

Third is the God of Action versus the God of Inertia. Elijah understood that the God of Israel was not an armchair figurine, remotely stationed in some distant place looking in on creation occasionally but never acting in history. Elijah believed in a God of action. He knew what God had done in the history of the Israelites. He knew God had brought them out of Egypt, brought them through the wilderness, took them over the Jordan into the promised land, helped them fight and vanquish their enemies, enabled them to form the new nation-state from the twelve tribes, and gave them the strength and wisdom to build the temple for God's glory. God is a God of action who would manifest God's power, presence, and majesty within human history.

This was not a god of inertia and apathy, a god of lethargy and antipathy. This God promised to act and make good on his promises. Elijah knew God's promise to Moses that "I will be with you." God would act in time and space, and his faith in God buoyed Elijah's conviction that God would do so.

When priests of Baal cried out and their god did not answer, they went into a spiritual tailspin because they knew the waiting would be a long time. Baal acted through the wind and storm but not through the faithful entreaties and prayers of his people.

We must remember that for our faith to work we must work our faith. God never said, "Blessed are the idle for I shall idle with them." The lexicon of faith is filled with action words, words that move, ideas and beliefs which transcend and transform people and circumstances because God is living and acting throughout creation. God is not an armchair, do-nothing, wait-and-see God. God is not a God of inactivity and inertia, but a God of action and trust; a God of deliverance; a God of liberation, conquest, and salvation!

We need God to act but God sometimes needs our action on God's behalf. "Who will go for me?" asks God. There comes a time when we must take our stand and stand our ground notwithstanding the odds, popular opinion, opposition, and pressure. Martin Luther finally said, "Here I stand." So did Paul Robeson and countless other saints, both men and women, across the ages who stood on their convictions, on unyielding faith, belief and absolute trust in God. They knew that God acted in human history, that God transversed the elements of time and space to make God's will known to God's people.

God expects this from us. God does not want us to dither, hesitate, hedge, and limp between two opinions. God has demonstrated this time and again in our lives, but we still need proof that God is God, that God will act and make good on God's promises by bringing us through. After all the hell and healing, the personal trials and tribulations, we still waver and equivocate between the ways of Baal or the ways of God. We still offer our bulls as excuses and not as genuine sacrifices and pieces of atonement so that God's will and work may finally prevail in our lives. How long shall we limp? When will we finally come into full realization that it is the God of Israel and Jesus Christ who have brought us, kept us, sustained us through the trials and storms of our spiritual journey? Elijah's mandate was finally to convince his people that they had better stop limping and start walking with confidence, trust, and faith in God!

How long will you limp between two opinions, people of God? It is time to take the moral high ground, to stand on the pinnacles of trust and confidence in God, to put the bulls aside, and to claim the God of Abraham, Isaac, and Jacob as the foundation to our hope and future as a people of God! How long will you limp? Amen!

They Didn't Have To Do It, But They Did

Corpus Christi   *Genesis 14:18-20*

Life is filled with stories of those selfless saints who have done the great things, made the great sacrifices and moved the boundaries of human reciprocity beyond their current constraints.

A friend shared with me his experience at getting a flat tire while traveling at night through Southern Georgia en route to Florida. He knew of black men being lynched on remote Southern roads and now he was stranded on a road at eleven o'clock at night. It was pitch black with no houses in sight, and he was filled with fear and trembling. Should he walk the back roads, not knowing where he was going? So he sat in his car, afraid for his life. Suddenly he saw approaching lights in his rear view mirror. Too fearful to get out of his car to wave the motorist down for help, he sat frozen in his seat. The car raced by him, then suddenly stopped, reversed itself and screeched back beside his car. Suddenly a light flashed in his eyes and he saw the faint silhouettes of three white men in the car. "Do you need any help?" cried a voice with a slow Southern drawl. My friend was petrified and couldn't respond. "Do you need any help?" cried the voice again. "What's wrong? Cat got your tongue? Wait here, nigger, we'll send you some help all right!" shouted the driver as they sped off.

My friend sat in his car not knowing if the men would come back to lynch him. What was a black man doing stranded on a road in Southern Georgia? Should he stay in the car or leave the car? Twenty minutes later a tow truck pulled alongside his car. A beefy, tobacco chewing, white man in a blue uniform got out of the truck and asked if he needed help. His car was then towed into a local gas station for repair. My friend got a room in a motel and had his car repaired the next day and then went on his merry way. The men who stopped didn't have to stop, but they did. They didn't have to send help, but they did. The tow truck man didn't have to come to the aid of my friend, but he did. The white mechanics didn't have to fix his car, but they did.

Life is filled with examples of people doing heroic deeds, the unexpected things, and our faith and confidence in human beings are once again restored. God puts such people in our lives to help us in times of great need.

In our scripture lesson we find Abram doing a heroic deed. After discovering that his nephew was captured he developed a rescue plan to save him and retrieve the goods and women confiscated in battle. Abram didn't have to do this, but he did it. Abram developed a rescue plan to save his nephew and his people.

God encourages the saints and heroes to develop a rescue plan for the perishing. Daniel's rescue plan had the jaws of the lion locked in a cage. God rescued Saul, the persecutor of Christians, and transformed him into the chief missionary for Christ. Shadrach, Meshach and Abednego were rescued from the fiery furnace, and David was rescued by Jonathan. David rescued the Israelites from the Philistines, and Moses rescued the Hebrews from Egyptian bondage. A ram rescued Abraham's sacrifice of his son Isaac, and Jesus rescues us from sin. Abram rescued his nephew and his people from persecution. He didn't have to do it, but he did. He risked his own life to save others.

The newspapers recently carried the story of a substitute firefighter from a small town in New York who jumped off Hudson Bridge to save the life of a woman committing suicide. The man seeing the woman dive off the bridge dove in after her at the risk of his own life. He didn't have to do it, but he did it. He rescued a dying woman.

What about the man in Detroit who recently rescued his family from a blazing house? Hearing the screams of his twelve-year-old daughter, he broke the back door down and saved her life amid a spiralling inferno of flames and smoke. He didn't have to save his daughter's life, but he did without regard for his own life. What inspires a man or woman to risk his or her own life to save another? There is something deep within that compels a person in a moment of compassion to help another in trouble.

Abram could have easily ignored the plight of Lot. He could have looked the other way, but he didn't. His compassion and concern moved him to action. So he trained 318 men who pursued their enemies until they were captured at Hobah. There they found the frightened women, seized the goods that were stolen, and gave them safe passage home. Abram cared about his people. He did the good deed because he had empathy for those in difficulty.

One man, who was rescued by another man from his burning car, said, "Thank you for going out of your way to help me." "That is my way," said the rescuer. "If I were in the same predicament I hope that someone would help me."

Helping others in critical times of need sustains our faith in humanity. A young man helps a blind man cross a busy Manhattan intersection. A young girl helps an elderly woman carry her groceries after her bags have burst in the parking lot. Two men come to the aid of a woman who was nearly raped by two other men.

The thieves who car-jacked another man's vehicle were hotly pursued by two citizens who saw the crime while at a stop light. The man whose car was stolen happened to be Caucasian. The pursuers happened to be African-American.

Fortunately, the annals of history are filled with people who do things they don't have to do, but in a moment of compassion and rage they come to the rescue of those in danger. Abram was one of those heroic persons of the Bible who would put his own life on the line to help save others.

After Abram rescued Lot and retrieved the stolen spoils, King Melchizedek of Salem did something he didn't have to do. He gave thanks to Abram by blessing him and by blessing the most high God who made the rescue possible.

I am reminded of the one leper who, after being healed by Jesus, returned and gave thanks for his blessing. King Melchizedek didn't have to say "thank you" to Abram but he did. So, delighted and overjoyed with Abram's heroics, he brought out bread and wine and blessed him and blessed God. Abram received a double blessing for his deeds.

It is important that we learn to say "thanks" to the people who go out of their way to perform the good deed and the heroic act. It is important that we thank them while they are living instead of after they die. Don't wait until they die to give them their roses. Give them now!

One elderly gentleman recalled with pain how he had found a little girl who had wandered away from her mother at the Michigan State Fair grounds. The man stayed with the hysterical girl for two hours until her mother could be located. The man was deeply hurt because the mother didn't even say "thank you" for finding her child and keeping her safe.

For countless blessings received we should learn to give thanks. One man, when writing his bills, always wrote "Thank you" in the memo line on his checks. When asked why he did this, he said, "It's just a blessing to have money for which to pay my bills. I am just grateful to God for this blessing."

Little things like giving thanks go a long way in fostering good will among fellow human beings. Melchizedek did not have to bless Abram, but he did. He had gratitude in his heart for what Abram did. The king could have easily ignored the heroics of Abram. He could have looked the other way and forgotten about Abram. But instead he expressed his gratitude for the blessings he received from Abram's deeds. Giving a blessing to Abram was the least thing he could do. Melchizedek didn't have to say "thank you," but he did.

The good Samaritan didn't have to rescue the man assailed by robbers on the Jericho Road, but he did. He didn't have to find a room in the inn and pay for his meals, but he did.

The apostle Paul did not have to risk life and limb to missionize parts of Asia Minor and other territories by starting new churches. He didn't have to brave insults, hardships, snakebites, shipwrecks, and virtual starvation, but he did. His love of Christ compelled him to do the implausible and achieve the impossible. Paul didn't have to go to jail, but he did. He didn't have to make such sacrifices for Christ, but he did.

Martin Luther King, Jr., Medgar Evers, and Malcolm X didn't have to give their lives for the black struggle for freedom, but they did! Rosa Parks didn't have to stand up by sitting down on a Birmingham bus and refusing to give her seat to a white man, but she did.

Likewise, the other disciples and apostles didn't have to take the crucible of faith and spread the Good News of Christ, but they did. Our world has been made better by people doing things they didn't really have to do.

The supreme sacrifice, however, was made by Christ himself. He didn't have to leave his carpenter's shop in Nazareth, but he did. He didn't have to take his ministry on the road, but he did. He didn't have to choose twelve disciples, but he did. He didn't have to feed the five thousand, but he did. He didn't have to heal the sick, cast out demons, make the lame walk and the mute talk, but he did.

It is because of Christ's sacrifices and his willingness to die for us that we have this life. Christ did not have to endure insults, but he did. He didn't have to teach and preach, but he did. He didn't have to give himself to be arrested and crucified, but he did. He didn't have to get up from the grave, but he did!

Christ went out of his way to show us another way, so that we might have a life filled with joy, gladness, and the positive pursuit of God's Word. The Word didn't have to become flesh in Christ, but it did. The early church did not have to survive the persecutions, but it did.

It is by faith and belief and trust in Christ that we are able to do what God calls us to do. God the Father did not have to give his only begotten son, but He did.

Our lives are made better because people do things on our behalf that they really don't have to do. The saints who pray for us in ministry don't have to do it, but they do. The people who take the time to say "thank you" in a job that is often thankless don't have to do it, but they do because of their love and appreciation for the minister's work.

As ministers of the Gospel we don't have to say "thanks," but we do because we appreciate the sacrifices of God's people: the long hours of volunteerism, the major sacrifices of time away from their families, the faithful witness they give to God in their lives, and the sacrifices of talent and treasures so the church might move forward. They don't have to do these things, but they do. Their love of God compels them to sacrifice and give their best for Christ as he has given his best for us.

We must thank God daily for people like Abram who will develop a rescue plan at the risk of their own lives to save others, and like Melchizedek who will take the time to say "thank you" for a job well done. They don't have to do it, but they do, and we thank God for their compassion, love, and empathy for people in need. We thank God for their blessings in our lives. We give honor and glory to God for their willingness to go out of their way to make life better for others. My friend who was stranded that night on that road in Georgia did a heroic thing. Although it took three months, he got the names of the people who "saved" him and sent them thank you cards for their assistance at a critical time of his life. Thank God for the people who do what they don't have to do, but do it anyway because of their faith and trust in God and their abiding, undying love for the people of God! Amen!

In Times of Need

Proper 5   *1 Kings 17:8-24*
Pentecost 3
Ordinary Time 10

She was worn and thin, a lonely woman solemnly gathering sticks in a lonely place. The yellow sun scorched the brown earth. It was a dry and desolate place. She had no fortune. She had no prospects for the future. As a widow she had no means of income save the occasional dole of the monarchy and her religious community. After gathering the sticks, she would then go home, kindle a small fire and cook a last jar of cornmeal and oil for her son and herself. She knew that she would soon die. Food had run out. Time had run out. The end was near and all hope for the future had died out. So she gathered her sticks for the last time. Tears welled in her eyes as she picked up the sticks one by one. She remembered the better times when her husband was alive, when food was plentiful and the family was in good health, but she kept gathering the wood until her arms were full.

Suddenly a voice whispered to her from a nearby bush, "Bring me some water so that I may drink." She paused, almost surprised, but without looking in the direction of the voice, and moved toward the well to bring the stranger water. "Bring me bread so I may eat," said the voice. The woman stopped. "I have no bread except the meal in this jar. I am gathering wood for a fire so that I may go home and cook it for my son so that we may die," said the woman bitterly.

"Do not worry. Do not be afraid. Go and do as you have said, but make me some cake of the cornmeal first and bring it to me. Afterwards make some for you and your son. For thus says your Lord God of Israel your jar of meal shall not be emptied and your jug of oil will not fail until the day that the Lord sends rain on the earth."

The woman did as she was asked. The stranger went home with her and they ate. She cooked the meal into cakes of bread and gave them to Elijah. Elijah ate and the food and jugs of oil never ran out. Although despondent, the widow trusted Elijah enough to respond obediently to his entreaties for help. Elijah did what God commanded. The widow did what Elijah asked and God brought forth prosperity out of a dire situation. It was a time of need for Elijah, as well as a time of need for the widow.

Several points are significant in this text about how God acts in times of great need.

At a time of desolation, God can bring consolation to those in need. In the midst of hopelessness, God can provide hope. The scriptures say there was drought in the land. There was not much food to eat. The inhabitants of the land prayed and prayed for rain, to no avail. The woman had lost her husband. Her son was "dead" and she had no prospects for the future. But even in her desolation God would bring consolation. In her hopelessness God would provide hope.

Now many interpret this text as the widow bringing consolation for Elijah. The truth is they each give consolation to the other in a time of critical need for both. They both did something which would ultimately make a difference in each of their lives. The widow gave what she did not have. Elijah went where he would not have gone otherwise and healed her sick son.

The widow virtually lost all hope. She was going home to die. Elijah was hungry and perhaps depressed. Elijah called to her and challenged her to raise her sights, to use what God had given her to help him, and by helping him she helped herself. What began as a journey of hopelessness for the widow ended as an experience of consolation. God can do this for us!

The man who has been told on his first visit to the doctor that the lump in his throat is a possible cancer is comforted in knowing on his second visit that the tumor is benign.

The family whose child has been missing for days is comforted in discovering that the child is alive and well.

These are people who begin their days without hope that they can ever make anything of their lives, but suddenly during the course of the day something happens which changes their prospects for the future. What began as desolation ends up as consolation. They started out with their sights so low but ended up with great expectations of themselves and God.

Then there are many people whose days are measured by lost causes and dashed dreams. They exist on slender threads of hope. They have come to the end of their ropes. We see evidence daily of people living on the jagged edges of despair, and many of them have fallen into the abyss of despair and hopelessness. We read of them in the newspaper. We hear their stories of despair and travail on the nightly news. Theirs is a canticle of sorrow, pain, and grief, and they have not received consolation from the Great Comforter.

We may begin our day in sadness, without hope, without prospects for a realizable future. Then suddenly the stranger shows up and provides comfort, and through it all God restores hope to a hopeless situation.

Howard Thurman shared the story of how dismayed he was in discovering that after all the fanfare about his going away to college, when he finally got to the railway station on his journey to Morehouse College, he did not have enough money to purchase a ticket. Too embarrassed to go home, he sat on the station stairs, sobbing uncontrollably. Suddenly a stranger appeared and asked him what he was crying about. "I don't have a ticket," said Thurman. "I'm supposed to be going to Morehouse College and now I can't go." "Oh hell," said the stranger. "I'll buy your ticket." Thurman never knew the man's name, but a moment of desolation was changed into consolation by a cigar-chomping railway worker who bought his ticket from Daytona Beach, Florida, to Atlanta, Georgia.

Both Elijah and the widow brought comfort to each other in a time of great need.

In a time of scarcity and dearth, God makes a provision. Elijah was hungry for food and the widow was hungry for a deeper faith and encouragement amid her troubles. Under every condition of scarcity God makes a provision. Sometimes God will provide new resources. At other times God will help us to see our current resources in a different light so they might be used in new ways. The widow had cornmeal and oil but could not make it last. She was living in a time of scarcity of material and spiritual resources.

In time of need Elijah was a godsend to her and she was a godsend to Elijah. How often have we found ourselves in situations where we are at the end of our resources, when we have exhausted the last vestiges of provision, and suddenly a miracle occurs and we are saved by the bell? Elijah experienced this when he was fed by the ravens in a cave.

One woman related the story of how she lost her job and was threatened with eviction. She was down to her last dollar and her children were hungry. Depressed and distraught, she seriously contemplated killing herself and her three children. She went to the mailbox thinking about how she would carry out her plan and suddenly found a check for five hundred dollars from an anonymous "friend" who had heard about her plight through another friend. In a time of scarcity, God made a provision. She later found work and is now happily supporting her family.

Once there was a church whose doors were threatened with foreclosure because they had difficulty paying their bills. The church was in dire financial straits. Someone did a newspaper article on how this church was in mission to the poor by feeding the hungry and clothing the naked. The church had gone into its operating budget to help people in need since its charitable contributions during the year had dropped drastically. People were impressed by how this church had faithfully and diligently helped those in need, even at the risk of having its own doors closed. Finally, letters poured in with contributions which eventually saved this church and its mission to the poor. A "day" that began in disconsolation and desolation ended in consolation.

History is replete with examples of provisions made at the last minute, bringing reprieve and newfound hope for people in despair. Although the widow was unaware, her fate would forever change with Elijah's intervention. He was just what she needed at a time of great need. Sometimes it is not what we have that determines our condition as much as how we use what we have that makes a difference. By exhorting her to convert the meal into cakes, Elijah taught the widow an important lesson in utility and provision.

At a time of cynicism and disbelief, God restored the optimism of faith and belief. Life's difficulties and hardships sometimes breed cynicism and a poverty of spirit. But sometimes a helping hand, a kind word, a gesture from a stranger can restore faith.

A friend related a story about how he lapsed into a state of depression after his mother died. While walking through the park with tears in his eyes he suddenly saw a baby crying loudly as he was carried by his mother. He and the baby locked eyes, as if suspended in time. The baby suddenly stopped crying and smiled. This smile was a confirmation that God still cared and that all would be well. His cynicism and anger with God for his mother's death was suddenly transformed into a renewed confidence in God. This friend realized that he was not alone and that God still cared for him. A baby's smile changed his disbelief into a feeling that God still loved him.

The widow had fallen on hard times. Her son was in a coma and near death. Her husband had died. She may have become cynical and bitter because of hard times. But Elijah restored her faith by reviving her son. Elijah transformed her cynicism into a newfound optimism. Food and oil, which had been scarce, became abundant. A son who was near death was now restored to health.

Along life's way we need these little victories, these triumphs of life and the Spirit, after being beaten down so long by life's trials and tribulations. Elijah himself may have had a reprieve of faith after his hard trials and struggles.

The truth is that whatever our condition, God meets us along the way to give us consolation, prosperity, hope, and faith amid our numerous concerns and struggles. Even when all seems lost, we must keep the faith, look up, and keep our eyes open for God's miraculous intervention. When all seems hopeless, that is when God shows up to restore hope and confidence. Whether it is Elijah for the widow or the widow for Elijah, God sends someone to us in times of need. God shows up in times of need and the faithful must keep trusting through the trials and storms of human experience. In times of need, we need God most. In times of need, we need others most. In times of need, others need us most! Amen!

Extreme Measures

Proper 6 *1 Kings 21:1-21a*
Pentecost 4
Ordinary Time 11

The tragedy of Naboth is a lesson in the lengths some leaders will go to have their way and maintain power. Theft of property, conspiracy, and assassination are a few of the diabolical machinations employed by some leaders to maintain control over their subjects. In our text today we find that Jezebel has plotted the death of a man named Naboth because he refused to give up his land to King Ahab so that the king might have a vegetable garden. The crimes of grand theft and murder over such a paltry thing as planting vegetables seem an extreme absurdity, but it is not unusual today where people are killed and kingdoms are toppled, where people murder loved ones to get the insurance payoff, and where others do anything to satiate their lust for greed.

The land was invaluable to Naboth because it was a gift from God and a family inheritance he did not want to surrender. But Ahab, annoyed with Naboth's decision, and after returning home from rebuke, moaned and complained to his wife Jezebel of the matter. She, with her devious heart, created a plot to have Naboth destroyed so his land might be confiscated. This story is a tragedy of great proportions because the theft and murder were entirely senseless, and because they were committed by leaders who were called to demonstrate moral fortitude and courage at a critical time in Israel's history. Ahab could have easily planted his garden elsewhere, but because of avarice in his heart, he could not bring himself to accept "no" for an answer. What began as a query for the purchase of land ended up as senseless homicide. What began as an effort in horticulture ended up as a felony murder in the first degree. Ahab and Jezebel utilized extreme measures to get their point across but had long lost their souls in the cauldrons of decadence and despair. What made their measures so diabolically extreme?

The first extreme measure was bringing false charges against Naboth. Because of his refusal to sell the land to King Ahab, Jezebel sat down and wrote a letter which would solicit the support of co-conspirators in her plot. They would falsely accuse Naboth of cursing God and king and would drum up support for his execution. By besmirching his character, the stage would be set for his murder. Law required that at least two witnesses be present who could bring accusation against the perpetrator. Jezebel arranged for two scoundrels to bring false charges against Naboth.

Naboth was honest about not wanting to sell his land, but Jezebel the liar transformed that honesty into deceit. She created the image of a man who cursed the king and subverted his policies. She invoked the name of God in her plot by accusing Naboth of cursing God. She left no stone unturned and no avenue unexplored in having him accused and tried in the court of public opinion to justify her connivance. The jealousy and rage which prompted this scheme exemplify the power of the demonic, which can twist and deform, and through the use of skulduggery and evil, destroy an innocent man's life.

How often have we heard the stories of those falsely accused and their accusers recanting?

The second extreme measure was that, after being falsely charged, Naboth was senselessly murdered. Slaughter of the innocent is not only a stigma of our modern times, but it also occurred in ancient history. Naboth was simply a citizen enjoying his rights. He wanted to keep his land because it meant something to him. He had inherited the land from his family, and since that land was a valuable commodity, he wanted to keep it, till its soil, and then pass it down to his children. His refusal of the king's offer was honest. He loved the land and wanted to keep it for posterity. King Ahab may have gone home, sulked, and eventually complied with Naboth's wishes, but his evil wife saw an opportunity to destroy a life and confiscate property. "How dare he refuse you, Ahab? You are the king and you must do what you please."

Lord Acton's statement that "Power corrupts and absolute power corrupts absolutely" is no misrepresentation. The issue here was power, and Jezebel was determined to use it to have her way even if it meant destroying the life of an innocent man. So she plotted to have Naboth assassinated by two scoundrels, after they had defiled and ridiculed him at a banquet! He would be shamed, defamed, then taken out into the town square and stoned to death for his insolence. This would be so the king could plant his vegetables!

The newspapers recently carried a story of a woman who was murdered in her house by teenagers. When asked why they murdered the old lady, the youngest boy, who was fourteen, said, "Because she would not give up the gold watch we wanted." A woman, who was the pillar of support in her community, was murdered because she refused to part with the precious gold watch handed down from two generations to her. Like Naboth, her refusal cost her her life. Another boy stated that she had pleaded with them to take whatever they wanted but not the gold watch. So they shot her three times in the head and took a watch which did not work.

Our lives are filled with stories of the slaughter of the innocent. We see daily the grim reminders of how greed, power, and corruption will cause people to kill for no reason. We see it personally, and we see it politically, as warring factions from Africa and America to the Middle East destroy innocent people for no earthly reason.

What made Ahab and Jezebel's crime so reprehensible and extreme is that they could have easily used other means of persuasion to get the land. Murder should not have been the first resort. More dialogue could have ensued and all parties could possibly have come to an amicable agreement.

In this life some people are too quick to kill in not having their way. Why must murder be the first resort when all other avenues of persuasion have not been pursued and exhausted?

The third extreme measure was that after being falsely accused and murdered, Naboth's land was quickly confiscated. After he was murdered, they took his land. They violated his inheritance, took his life, and confiscated his land. They might have entered an agreement to lease his land, but instead they stole it from him.

Why couldn't they have entered into negotiations, given their power and resources? Why couldn't they have provided a more lucrative alternative that would persuade Naboth to let them use the land?

Too often we have heard these stories of land confiscated and stolen from Native Americans to blacks in Oklahoma where black landowners were murdered and run off their land when oil was discovered. Sadly, history is filled with stories of people having to flee and give up their land because of the greed of those in power!

They seized Naboth's land and killed him. They stole his birthright inheritance. They went to extremes to have their way. They had no shame. Poor Naboth had no one to defend him. No one would come to his aid. The conspirators had no compunctions in taking his life. Who would defend him? How would his death be avenged? His family would forever live with the memory of their loved one being falsely accused then executed like a common criminal. Who would mourn and weep for them?

How often we cringe at the slaughter of those innocents who have never been avenged nor their assailants brought to justice. But who was powerful enough to battle the king and queen in court? Who was man enough to call them out for their sordid actions?

Enter Elijah the prophet! After hearing of the insidious plot, Elijah, commanded by God, and being a man of courage and boldness, confronted Ahab for his crime. Here the prophet confronts the king on behalf of the innocent, on behalf of truth and justice. Now Elijah the Tishbite would pronounce God's judgment on King Ahab: "Thus says the Lord. In the place where dogs licked up the blood of Naboth, dogs also lick up your blood." Because you have shed innocent blood your blood will be shed. The prophet has thus spoken in the name of the Lord and justice and recompense will be exacted for this awful crime.

The crime? Ahab was too weak a man to do the right thing in the eyes of God. He, like Shakespeare's Macbeth, succumbed to the machinations of a villainous wife. Ahab knew better, but allowed himself not to know the truth of Naboth's demise. He pretended not to know, knowing full well that his wife had malevolently planned the debacle from start to finish.

We thank God for the saints of justice, undaunted and bold, who come forth and speak the truth on behalf of the innocent. They are unafraid of the repercussions of power, but possess the strength and resolve to be advocates for human justice. Such persons put their lives on the line for love, truth and freedom. They know the hazards of the undertaking, but they speak for God and claim his promises for victory. They are men and women who do not shirk the awesome task of exacting justice and speaking truth to the powerful.

Elijah was courageous in his confrontation of King Ahab. He prophesied that Ahab, too, would meet an awful end for his evil deeds. We might say that Elijah also went to extreme measures in bringing judgment on Ahab. Here was one man with limited resources. He had no armies that marched by day and by night. He had no arsenal of deadly weapons with which to vanquish enemies. He had no judiciary system which could manipulate the processes of justice in his favor. He did not have gangs of men and mercenaries anxious to do battle on his behalf. All he had was God on his side. Here was one man who stood up for another man and brought truth to judge the people responsible for his death.

Elijah had God on his side, the God of Abraham, Isaac and Jacob. He could stand for truth and justice because God gave him the volition and courage to speak. Ahab was undoubtedly startled and surprised at the force of Elijah's judgment. He could scarcely believe that such extreme judgment would be pronounced on his extreme measures. Extreme measures must be brought to extremes for justice to prevail.

Because of the force of Elijah's judgment and his conviction of conscience, Ahab tore off his clothes and humbled himself before God. God, being pleased with his humility, spared him for a time, and the wrath would be brought down on a future generation.

The point here is that in this world of extreme measures where the slaughter of the innocent is as common as the air we breathe, where the innocent are unjustly tried and executed, where people are living in communities and families under siege in fear of their lives, where the common man is afraid to bring truth to powers which have corrupted themselves and have instilled so much fear that people are afraid to take a stand, we need extreme measures of courage, fortitude, faith, tenacity, resolve, and justice to balance the ledgers of untruth and injustice in the land. We need a prophetic voice to counter the corruption of silence in the face of evil.

We need people of the Christ spirit, the spirit of Elijah, who can stand unafraid before the solemn assemblies, the power brokers, and the establishment of society, and speak the words of justice and truth. These are men and women who have broken the spell of silence, the yoke of discouragement and humiliation. They stand for God. They speak the things of God without regard to the consequences. They do it because it is right and just and true. They put their lives on the line because they love the Lord. They love the people of God and they abhor oppression and injustice in whatever forms or colors they manifest themselves.

A single voice crying for truth can make a difference in our world, whether it is the truth of injustice, oppression, physical and emotional abuse, theft, corruption, or the murder and slaughter of the innocent. This is the spirit of Elijah and this is the spirit of Christ. We thank God for the indomitable spirit of courage which dares to stand for love, truth and justice! Man's extremities are God's opportunities for those who are willing to stand for God however extreme the measure! Amen!

Nowhere to Run, Nowhere To Hide

Proper 7 **1 Kings 19:1-15a**
Pentecost 5
Ordinary Time 12

After predicting a drought, raising the widow's son at Zarephath, challenging and slaying the prophets of Baal, Elijah the prophet is now on the run for his life from Queen Jezebel and King Ahab. Buoyant, strong, and confident, he has stood toe to toe with the powers that be, denouncing every evil. He has bravely articulated divine intentions, but now we find him fleeing for his life to Mount Horeb.

See him now cowering in a cave hewn in the mountain's side, depressed and weary, afraid for his life. Elijah now realizes the magnitude and implications of the things he has done. That one man could undertake such enormous responsibility has caused him to take inventory of himself, his relationship with God, and the deeper meaning of his own life.

The prophet has done a magnificent thing, but now he must hide out in the cave for reprieve and solace, for comfort and restoration of his own soul. He has no friends to comfort him. He is alone and afraid. Ultimately though, he realizes that there is nowhere to run and nowhere to hide. He can run to the crevice in the mountain's side, but he cannot hide from the truth of his life and the reality of God, who is still presently directing his every step.

We, too, like Elijah may find ourselves on the run, seeking refuge in some remote and distant place. We may be on the run from the painful reality of past mistakes and difficulties. We may be on the run from others whom we have threatened and who make us insecure. We may be on the run from God and even ourselves. The truth is we can run from these things but we can't hide from them. They are forever with us. They are part of our very nature and being. They tell us why we are and who we are. There is always that part of our past which catches up with us, where we come to a deeper realization of what we have done to ourselves and others. It is a place of reckoning, a time of going deeper, a time of coming clean to ourselves in order to be who we really are and assess what it all means. They are the "Jacob at the River Jabbock" moments; our "Daniel in the Lions' Den" moments; our "Paul on the Damascus road" experiences and our "Elijah in the cave" moments, where we wrestle with the truth of who we are and what we have done. The realization of our deeds often leaves us feeling alone, despondent and depressed. In coming to the realization of truth, we may even feel that God has abandoned us and that there is really nowhere to run and nowhere to hide.

Elijah felt this way and we might feel this way. The truth is we can run, but we can't hide. The reminders are always there, but God is present to help us through those moments of indiscretion and indecision, where we feel stagnant and alone, without rudder or anchor in the storms of life.

Several truths I wish to reveal in this text as it relates to Elijah and our own experience as human beings.

First, we can run from others, but we can't hide from ourselves. Elijah infuriated Jezebel and Ahab because of the slaughter of the prophets of Baal. Elijah publicly exposed the fraudulent aspects of Jezebel's religion and brought shame and disgrace on the monarchy. Elijah was commanded by God to confront and destroy the prophets, but Jezebel and Ahab put out a contract on his life. So fearing for his life, Elijah ran from himself, others, and God!

He could run from them, but he could not hide from himself. Elijah realized that it was God who commanded and commissioned him to challenge the authority of the king and queen. It was God who called him to a task. He realized that while God commanded him to destroy the prophets of Baal, it was Elijah who had to take ultimate responsibility for what had happened.

A similar truth can be applied to Jacob. He could run from Esau for stealing his birthright, but he could not hide from himself. He could not avoid the fact that it was he and no other who had committed this travesty against his own flesh and blood.

There are moments in our lives when we come to the painful realization of who we are, what we are, and what we have done. We can run from others, but we cannot escape ourselves and our own responsibility in the matter. We experience our fall from grace through the burdensome realization that what we have done has hurt others and hurt them deeply, and in a larger sense brought sorrow and tragedy upon them and upon ourselves.

In his book *The Fall,* Nobel Prize winning author Albert Camus tells the story of Jean Baptist-Clamence, who falls from grace in his realization that he is not the man he has pretended to be to others around him. He has played the role and worn the mask, but suddenly, while gazing at himself in the mirror, he realizes the true Clamence is the "lowest of the low" of men.

Perhaps Elijah felt that he was the lowest of the low. Although he had done what God commanded, which was true and righteous, perhaps the truth of what he had done to the prophets of Baal and to Ahab and Jezebel came crashing in on him. Perhaps he realized that even as a man of God called to do God's bidding, there were dire consequences and possible recriminations and repercussions which would come from others as a result of what he did. Elijah could run from Ahab and Jezebel, but he could not escape the truth of what *he* did to incur their wrath and scorn.

There are countless individuals who run from others but cannot hide from themselves. A boy I grew up with was recently arrested for murdering his uncle. He had been on the run for one year and finally the truth of what he had done caught up with him. He could run from the police but he could not hide from himself. His moment of truth was when "I realized that I had killed my *mother's* brother."

Try as we may to run from others, we know what we have done. The truth of our deeds pierces us at the core of our being and we cry out for help and mercy. We are suddenly alone in our realization that what we have done has adversely affected others and their lives will forever be impacted because of it. We can no longer suppress the grim reality of what we have done. We can no longer run from the truth.

Second, we can run from our actions but we can't hide from their consequences. For every action there is a reaction. For every action there are consequences for those actions. Elijah may have suddenly realized that he would have to pay a price for action even as a man of God. Even in the things of God there are consequences for our work. In speaking God's truth, we often incur the wrath, envy, and malice of others. There are consequences for our actions that are often difficult to face. We may not come into the full force of those actions until we are alone and have time in our lives to think them thoroughly through!

Elijah fled because he realized that he would have to pay a price for his action and that payment could well be his own life. The deed had been done and now would come the payment for that deed. Elijah fled because he may not have realized that even in the things of God there had to be a measure of human and personal responsibility for his actions in relation to other people. It was Elijah that Ahab and Jezebel wanted to kill, not God. He could not do the things of God, blame them on God, and then expect God to make reparations for his action. This may have been the thing which depressed Elijah. Although he knew of God's miraculous power of intervention and intercession on behalf of God's appointed and anointed, he may have suddenly realized that he would have to pay up personally for those things executed on behalf of God. He could run from the deed, but he could not hide from the consequences and his personal responsibility for what had happened.

Too often in life we try to escape responsibility for our actions. We blame it on God. The lady who dropped her six-month-old infant out of a fifth-story apartment window said that God commanded her to do it. We know of countless instances of people putting total blame and responsibility on God so as to evade personal responsibility for the consequences of their actions. At some point in our journey, we must realize that there will be a price that we must pay personally for the things we do in this life. "Take whatever you want out of this life and pay for it." Elijah came to that realization. While he hid in a cave, he could not escape knowledge that there would be real, material consequences for his actions.

Serving and speaking for God often means risking persecution, prosecution, and even death itself. The realization can bring despondency and depression. We feel like hiding out in a cave from the rest of the world, never to be seen or heard again. This is the comforting way out of such dilemmas, but a time comes when we must face the music, bear our cross, and carry the crucible of responsibility for our actions.

Third, we can run for our lives, but we can't hide from God who gives us that life. We can run into the darkness of a cave, but we can't hide from the searchlights of God that seek us!

What a relief to know that the love, truth, and goodness of God will search us out wherever we are and whatever we have done! Elijah was relieved to know that while he was alone God had not abandoned him. God was still present with him and God understood the pain, doubt, fear, and uncertainty he had about his future. Powerful adversaries had issued death threats, and Elijah had to find solace. God would hide him in the shadow of his wings. God would provide his soul with a place of rest and convalescence after all he had been through.

God's love and goodness are like searchlights in the dark shadows. There Elijah sat alone in the dark, cold with fear, trembling at the thought of both the magnitude and consequences of his actions, but God spoke to him providing solace and comfort. God's words quietly reassured Elijah that God was ever with him, and that he would not be left alone to die at the hands of his enemies.

If we faithfully serve God, we may fall on tough times. We may feel the wrath of God's adversaries crashing in on us. We may feel at times that we are alone, in our solitary rooms and caves, hiding out from all that is and all that will be. But God never fails. The love and mercy of God will seek us out. The voice will speak to us, "What are you doing here? ... Go out and stand, stand up ... What are you doing here? Go the way you came."

There are times in our lives when we have felt we have run the race and served God with all our strength, might, and heart. Then we find ourselves, like Elijah, hiding out in fear and fatigue. It may have been a sermon we preached which raised the ire of certain people in our churches. It may be the truth we spoke to others who were trying to deceive us. It may be the things we have done and said in the name of God which bring their own judgment and consequences which alienate and sequester us from those we are called to serve. We feel so all alone and God says, "What are you doing here? Get up and stand up and go and do as I have asked."

Nowhere to run. Nowhere to hide. When the painful truth of past actions comes crashing in on us, we can run, but we can't hide. When the memory of past mistakes catches us at a time of sheer vulnerability, we can run, but we can't hide. When our adversaries and enemies seek to assail us, we can run, but we can't hide. We can run from ourselves in fear of ourselves or run from others in fear of them, but the goodness and love of God will seek us out. We cannot hide from the presence and love of God. It will seek us out wherever we are. In our pain and sorrow, in our fear and despair, the love of God will find us in our caves of doubt, distrust, and uncertainty.

Elijah realized this at this moment when he felt lower than low. We may feel it in moments where we feel lower than low. The comfort is that we cannot hide from God. We cannot escape God's ubiquitous presence. God's love and concern will search us out and restore us to stand to face an unknown future. In our darkness, the light of God will find us. In our pain, the balm of God will soothe us. In our moments of deepest humiliation and despair, the spirit of God will lift us. "What are you doing here? Stand up and go the way you came!"

Elijah realized that he could run but he couldn't hide because the love of God was everywhere and would never let him go. As one of God's anointed, who obediently and faithfully responded to God's will and work, Elijah's experience in the darkened cave should be an ever present reminder of the goodness of God despite our pain, peril, and human predicament.

"Truth forever on the scaffold. Wrong forever on the throne, Yet, that scaffold sways the future, and behind the dim unknown, standeth God within the shadow, keeping watch above his own." Amen!

A Double Dose

Proper 8 *2 Kings 2:1-2, 6-14*
Pentecost 6
Ordinary Time 13

Anyone coming into contact with Elijah could see the full power of God's anointing on his life. Elisha would be next in line to continue Elijah's prophetic ministry and he knew the requirements of this awesome task. Elisha could not do it alone. The full anointing of God's spirit had to be in his life in order for him to succeed in his ministry, so Elisha asked that he receive a double portion of Elijah's spirit. Elisha felt the need for a second touch of Elijah's power and spirit because he knew what Elijah had been through, as had all the prophets before him. He knew the tenacity, resolve, strength, and courage exemplified by the great prophet in facing the prophets of Baal, confronting Ahab, and being a fugitive from the "miscarried justice" of Jezebel and Ahab. He knew that God had been with Elijah, and Elisha wanted a double dosage of that powerful spirit. Elisha was astute enough to know that his power to carry out his mission and ministry would have to come from on high. So he asked for the double portion and received it before Elijah's ascension.

Why did Elisha ask for this double portion of Elijah's spirit?

The double dose would consummate his commission as Elijah's successor. As a young man faced with the dangers and challenges of leadership during troubled times, Elisha needed to feel that his commission was consummated. He needed the spiritual reassurance. Having spent time with Elijah, and having witnessed the challenges to his ministry, he had to have absolute confidence and assurance that he was doing the right thing.

The commission would then be more than a verbal caveat, more than a laying on of hands. Elisha had to feel in his heart and soul that the commission for his leadership would be consummated. What better way than a double dose of the prophet's spirit?

In our journey of faith we sometimes need the affirmation and confirmation, the laying on of hands and the spiritual reassurance that we are doing the right thing and going in the right direction. Christ touched the blind man twice so he could see clearly. We too need the reassurance that a second touch or a double dosage brings in our service to the people of God.

Even though we have been called and anointed of God for this mighty work, there are times when we need a double portion of the Holy Spirit. There are moments when the Spirit's outpouring suffices to give us the assurance that what we are doing is pleasing in God's eyes.

There is nothing wrong with a double dosage. Sometimes we need the second touch or the second hug. Our hearts rest in quiet assurance that there is a higher power anointing our steps, directing our thoughts and sanctioning our actions on behalf of the Kingdom. Sometimes our windows, so filled with the debris and fog of both outside and inside concerns, need to be wiped more than once for us to see clearly. Elisha needed the assurance that his commission was being consummated, and a double portion of Elijah's spirit would provide a kind of blessed assurance for his ministry.

Second, a double dose would give Elijah strength to fight his adversaries. The office and responsibility of prophecy is no cakewalk. Elisha would have to be strengthened to fight the good fight. He would need a double portion of the Spirit to fortify his resolve in facing known and unknown enemies. He would need the strength to do battle against the adversaries of God. Who among us does not need the strength that a second portion gives? When souls are weary from doing battle against Satan, when minds are cloyed and hearts are besieged with lethargy and listlessness, a second portion of the spirit will provide the extra strength needed to fight the good fight.

God help those weary souls seeking to do battle against the enemy who have not been prayed up and strengthened for the fight. God help those entering the fray against Satan without the full power and anointing of God's Spirit. Prophecy is no easy thing. It requires the strength to stand before the solemn assemblies, to make judgments and pronouncements of God's condemnation against the woes and sins of humankind. It often means standing alone against a frightened and embittered majority. It often means putting one's life on the line for love, truth, and justice. Prophecy requires undaunted strength and power, an iron will, the wit and nerve to risk all so that others might have all. Elisha understood what would be required of him and knew that he needed more than mere human strength to fight the enemy. A double dosage of Elijah's spirit would give him the added strength to stand against the adversaries of Israel and God.

Elisha was very clever. He had studied his predecessor. He knew the hazards of the prophetic undertaking. He knew what would be required. He knew that prophecy often meant standing alone, without the benefit of standing armies that march by day and night. It would mean living as a force of one for God.

Elisha wanted to stay around Elijah as long as he could. He needed more time with his mentor so his spirit could rub off on him. He did not want Elijah to make the ascension until he had received the full dosage of strength needed for the fight. He needed confidence. He needed strength. He needed the added time that only a true mentor could give.

There are times in this life when we need a second dosage to provide us with strength for the fight.

A friend related a story to me about how his mother would keep him in church all day Sunday. This friend had come to loathe church because it took too much of his time. But as he had grown older, he realized the value of the lessons imparted to him as a youngster. "My mother stayed in church all day because she realized what she needed to fight the enemy and raise seven children alone. My mother stayed in church so she could get as much of the Holy Spirit as she could to raise us right and give us what we needed so we could grow into healthy, strong, and productive citizens of our community."

This friend realized the value of getting a double portion of the Holy Spirit and the full power of God's anointing in church "all day Sunday." Even if it meant hanging around the church so that the Spirit could bless, guide and empower a little longer, it was all necessary to garner strength to fight the enemy. Keeping them in church was his mother's way of making sure her children received a double, triple and quadruple portion of the Holy Spirit. She knew her children would need this to face the challenges of their lives.

How many of God's people have fallen from God's grace because they had not received a double portion of God's spirit to strengthen them for the fight? Had they prayed a little longer, tarried in the Spirit a little longer, studied the Word a little longer, fasted a little longer, praised God for blessings a little longer, given their services to the church a little longer, invoked the presence and power of God a little longer, they may have had just a little more strength to do battle against the enemy. Perhaps if they had just gotten a second portion, a double dose of the Spirit, they could have vanquished the thing they were facing!

We all need strength to be the people of God and to do God's will and work. We all need a double dosage of the Holy Spirit as a minimum daily requirement. We all need the wonderful outpouring of the Holy Spirit in our lives so that we might become living testimonies to the triumphant spirit of Christ!

Just as the adversaries of God hunted and attempted to kill the prophets, we, too, as the people of God must be prepared to fight against him with all that we have. In this fight we cannot afford to grow weak and weary but must muster the strength which will help us to win out over the forces of evil and destruction.

Third, a double dose would cleanse his soul and sustain his ministry over the long term. Perhaps there was fear and trembling and sickness unto death. Perhaps the prophet was unsure of what the future would hold. Thus a certain anxiety prevails; a nervousness or trepidation casts its shadow over the prophet. Elisha needed a spiritual elixir, a kind of internal cleansing of his soul, to purify him so he could sustain his ministry over the long haul.

Prophets easily burn out from overwork. The load they carry is tremendous. As ministers of the Gospel we, too, risk the reality of burnout. We are tired and burdened. We cannot bring ourselves to sustain our ministries over the long haul. We are worn out. The last vestiges of strength and stamina are sapped by the daily round of church life. We need a double dose to sustain us, to quicken our resolve, to re-energize us when limbs palsy and bones are brittled and wearied. This requires a kind of catharsis, a cleansing of the soul, a revitalization of the Spirit so we might continue the tasks God sets before us.

How many of us have petered out or fallen exhausted at critical times in our service to God? The spirit is willing but the flesh is weak. We pull ourselves out of bed to preach. We saunter to our meetings, with hearts heavy with woe and sadness. We are met continually by the constant and insatiable demands of our parishioners. But we need the "still water" moments, the "Gethsemane" moments, the "by the river" moments, where our souls are cleansed and our bodies are restored to a fresh vitality. The very thought of our weariness, that we might not have stamina to sustain ourselves over the long haul brings a kind of angst, an anxiety which does not easily dissipate. So we need a soul cleansing. We need to be renewed and refreshed to sustain our mission. We need not only strength to do battle but also a double dose of the Spirit to sustain us through the ups and downs, the volatilities and vicissitudes of our service for Christ!

By pouring out his concern to Elijah and pleading for a second portion of his spirit, Elisha was preparing to sustain himself, to run and finish the race.

In reading the diaries of John Wesley, we find that he had incredible stamina, traveling thousands of miles on horseback to bring the Word of God to the people of God. He needed a double dose of the Holy Spirit to move him through the trials, tribulations, and hardships of ministry.

Equally significant are the biographies of the early circuit riders on the American frontier. They were preachers of the Gospel who took the Word of God to dangerous and remote settlements of Europeans. Many of them lost their lives. Those who survived needed stamina and strength to sustain themselves through the harsh and brutal winters as well surmount the onslaught of an often faceless enemy. They needed a double dose of God's spirit to bravely preach the Word to the people of America.

One Methodist circuit rider had ridden so long in inclement weather that he was frozen dead to his saddle as he entered a small town in northern Minnesota. But many of them survived and succeeded in winning souls to Christ. The Great Awakening is a testament to the courage, energy and determination of those early Christian missionaries.

We today need a soul cleansing. We need to empty ourselves so the Spirit of Christ may be fully poured into us so we may continue our service to God and the church. Just as a double dose of the prophet's spirit would enable Elisha to face and overcome the perils and uncertainties of doing God's work, we today need a double dose of the Spirit of Christ. Wherever we serve we still need the second touch, a double portion and helping of the Holy Spirit. Without this anointing we cannot run the race, we cannot overcome the barriers and constraints, we cannot convict and convince souls to Christ unless the anointing is on our lives.

That's what it is really all about, getting a double portion of the Spirit's anointing so that we might be equipped to serve the people of God. We need a double dose today, in our homes, on our jobs, in our communities, in the nation at large, and even perhaps in the world itself.

We need strength and stamina for the fight, for the long haul, and a double dose of the Holy Spirit will help us through. Anyone serving the people of God must be equipped to do God's work over the long haul. We need, like Elisha, a double portion of God's spirit to help us in tough times.

We cannot do without it. The Lord's work is never finished. Like Elisha this double dose will consummate our commission, give us strength to do battle and sustain us through the ups and downs of serving the people of God. Have you received your minimum daily requirement of a double dose of Christ? God's full power and anointing is waiting to be poured out on you. Like Elisha, keep asking for the double dosage. Keep asking for God's anointing on your life. Keep asking for the Holy Spirit to come and fall fresh upon you like fresh, rushing rains. Keep asking for God's guidance and anointing as you seek to serve God and the people of God! Amen!

What Money Can't Buy

Proper 9 **2 Kings 5:1-14**
Pentecost 7
Ordinary Time 14

Naaman was the commander of the army of the king of Aram. He was a good, upstanding, and righteous man; a great warrior who had fought and won many battles and thus earned the respect of his master. But he had one problem which plagued him and caused him to be an outcast. He was a leper and he needed a cure. He was a great man, like many great men, with a flaw. Here was a fearless warrior who bore the telltale marks of the infirm and afflicted.

After asking his king if he could go and see the prophet Elisha, he was granted permission and set out on his journey with ten talents of silver, six thousand shekels of gold and ten sets of garments. As a respectable gentleman warrior, he would pay for his medicine. He would give the prophet a monetary reward for services rendered.

Notwithstanding his desire to pay the prophet, Naaman would soon realize that he would receive something that money could not buy.

Money did not buy a servant's disclosure of someone who could heal Naaman's leprosy. How paradoxical that a servant girl captured in the one of the raids of the Arameans would approach

Naaman's wife with information about a prophet who could cure her husband's leprosy. This information was undoubtedly unsolicited. The servant girl was captured in battle. She was a vanquished spoil of conquest. She didn't have to share her knowledge about Elisha's healing powers. She could have easily kept such knowledge to herself. As property of the conqueror, her bitterness could have prompted her to bask in Naaman's misery. As retribution for being taken captive and being powerless to redress her condition, she could have watched him suffer day by day, delighting in his affliction and viewing it as a kind of perverse payback for taking her prisoner.

However, empathy and compassion provoked her to share what she knew with Naaman's wife. All the money in the world could not buy this valuable information. All the money in the world could not have compelled this servant girl to come forward with an answer to the suffering of a fellow human being. Naaman no doubt would have gladly paid for such, but it was the kindness and goodness of a servant girl that would change his life for ever.

Valuable information is traded for large sums of money in the world marketplace of ideas every day. People often give their lives to receive a cure for disease or affliction. One man spent his life savings to receive information about a cure for AIDS. His search for a remedy had prompted him to pull out all stops in an effort to save his life. Sadly, he had come to realize that even his life's savings weren't enough to reveal information about a cure, but, ironically, he stumbled across some invaluable information quite by accident. Overhearing a conversation between two gay people in a restaurant, he discovered that different formulas for cures were being aggressively pursued in other countries. This was information received that money could not buy. This young man is now actively pursuing a cure for his condition in another country.

Sometimes valuable information comes to us which can save our lives and money cannot buy it. Sometimes such information comes from the most implausible sources. It comes in a twinkling of an eye, virtually unsolicited. The great cures of modern medicine have often come in this unexpected manner. Scientists and researchers labor for years for answers to life's most devastating and perplexing diseases and then suddenly the answer comes. All the money in the world could not buy the answer and it is only by the grace of God that the answer has come.

Money did not buy the servant girl. Money did not buy her desire to end her master's suffering. Money did not buy her willingness to share valuable information which would ultimately save Naaman's life. Money did not buy her sympathy, empathy and concern for another human being.

In this world of the Faustian impulse, where people will sell their souls to the devil on a whim for momentary pleasure, the fact that people are still willing to share something that money cannot buy gives us all hope. For there is a vestige of people who will help others because it is the right and just thing to do. They are not seeking financial compensation. They are not looking to be paid, but they do it out of altruism, love, and compassion for others. All the money in Naaman's account could not have purchased such knowledge from the servant girl.

Money did not buy the prophet's knowledge of healing. We know from our readings on leprosy that lepers were always in search of healing for their disease. As one of the most dreaded infirmities in ancient times, it often created social ostracism and contempt. Lepers were colonized or quarantined in certain areas of a city or town. Taboos against prolonged contact with lepers were very strong. That Naaman enjoyed his status as a great warrior is perhaps unusual for lepers, since they were often isolated from other segments of the community. Thus we can surmise that Naaman, like other lepers of his time, was desperately in search of a cure for his malady.

After hearing about the prophet, he travels to him, taking large amounts of money to pay him for services rendered. It is obvious that Naaman believed that Elisha would administer some hands-on cure for him, that Elisha's intervention and intercession would be personal. Naaman had already formulated in his mind the method of healing Elisha would prescribe. The scriptures say that Naaman believed Elisha would wave his hand over the spot (2 Kings 5:11). Perhaps Elisha would dispense some mysterious herb, spice or balm by externally applying it to the skin of Naaman. Perhaps he would put Naaman under a spell or trance and administer some internal potion, and after awaking from days of sleep, he would be miraculously cured. It is obvious that Naaman had some idea in his mind of the prophet's method for curing, otherwise he would not have been so displeased with what he found upon his arrival at the prophet's home.

Upon his arrival, Naaman was deeply angered when the prophet would not even come out of his house to greet him. He was incensed and insulted that the prophet would dismiss him in such a frivolous and discourteous manner. "What is this? I thought he would come out and wave his hand over the spot and call on the name of the Lord," said Naaman. He did not realize that the prophet knew something, that he was aware of a method of healing which surpassed all others. Naaman did not realize that the prophet was in possession of a deep secret that money could not buy; a secret revealed only by the power and spirit of a great and mighty God.

"Tell him to go dip in the Jordan River seven times," said Elisha. Enraged and perturbed, Naaman went down to the Jordan River, immersed himself seven times and was cured.

The prophet knew something Naaman did not know. The prophet shared a method of healing that money could not buy. Because Elisha was anointed of God, he was aware of how God could provide different methods of healing for all manner of diseases. Just as Elisha did not pay for such knowledge, Naaman could not buy it with all his money and worldly wisdom.

The prophet had come into a full awareness of the healing powers of the Jordan River. He could have only known this by the Spirit of God. The Spirit discloses knowledge of truth rarely possessed by human minds. Naaman never could have conceived of such a mundane cure because it was revealed only to the prophet and man of God. It was a unique method of healing that could easily have been taken for granted. The apparent frivolity of the method is evident in Naaman's contempt at the suggestion to dip himself into the Jordan seven times. This method of being cleansed and healed was not a standard prescription for leprosy. But it was a method of healing that money couldn't buy!

In a world where money buys virtually everything, even doctors with expert knowledge who can effect healing, it still, as in the case of Elisha and Naaman, could not buy a cure.

Money did not buy the miracle of Naaman's healing. What occurred was essentially a miracle. Naaman's healing by dipping in the River Jordan was a great blessing. Perhaps he had passed through those waters as many of his people before him. The river Jordan has spiritual significance in the life of the Israelite people. It is a place of crossing over into the new land, a place of healing, restoration, and renewal. The significance of that river in the life of the Israelites cannot be taken for granted. For this same reason, it also may have been held in a contempt which results from familiarity. It was a river that had always been there. It was taken for granted. The people had crossed its borders so many times and had become so familiar with it that for some it lost its symbolic and spiritual significance. This was probably true of Naaman, who was enraged at hearing of Elisha's suggestion.

But the miracle occurred. Despite his contempt, Naaman did what he was told and was cured of his leprosy. The miracle was of God. The prophet acted as an intermediary in that miraculous event.

Elated with his cure, Naaman offered Elisha money for his services but was refused because the prophet had something that money could not buy. We understand that Naaman wanted to pay him as a token of his appreciation for what Elisha had done. This was a perfectly normal and good thing to do, but Elisha refused the money because deep down he had something that money could not buy.

The deeper lessons of this text tell us that both Naaman and Elisha had something that money could not buy. Note that there was no personal intercession by the prophet on behalf of Naaman, but rather instructions and directions on what to do and where to go for the cure. Naaman's obedience to the prophet's command is equally something that money cannot buy. The prophet gave the instruction and the client responded in spite of his reservations about those instructions.

Thus money did not buy a servant's information. Money did not buy the prophet's knowledge of the cure. Money did not buy the miracle of the cure. Money did not buy Naaman's faith in doing what the prophet commanded.

Accordingly, there are many things in this world that money cannot buy. Money can buy companionship, but money cannot buy friendship. Money can buy a physician, but money can't buy good health. Money can buy medical expertise, but money can't buy a cure for disease. Money can buy a house, but money can't buy a home. Money can buy information, but money can't buy knowledge. Money can solicit loyalties, but money cannot buy obedience. Money can buy good works, but money can't buy faith.

All the characters of this story had something that money cannot buy. The servant girl had compassion. The wife of Naaman had loyalty. The prophet had knowledge. The River Jordan had the cure, and Naaman had the willingness and faith to be healed. All of these things money could not buy.

It is refreshing to know that there are still things in this world money cannot buy. Elisha refused to be monetarily paid for his services because of his relationship with God and also because there are some things in life upon which a monetary value cannot be placed. These are invaluable, priceless things: the look on the face of a child who has been healed, the smile of an adult who has been miraculously cured of cancer, the joy of a family in having a sick loved one restored. There is a realm of existence that is so profound and utterly amazing that we cannot put a price on it.

The prophet Elisha was well aware that what he had and shared with Naaman could not be sold for a price, could not be bought at a price. It is something deep within the human soul and spirit which delights and rejoices in caring and sharing and helping others. It cannot be purchased at any cost. This special something which runs from heart to heart and soul to soul is the love that God has for us and our love of others, which makes the difference in this life. We can all be instruments of God's healing for others, but that healing comes from a desire to heal and a willingness to be healed. This is something we can never put a price on because it is something that money cannot buy. Amen!

A Tale Of Two "Cities"

Proper 10 **Amos 7:7-17**
Pentecost 8
Ordinary Time 15

"**It** was the best of times. It was the worst of times ... It was an age of belief. It was an age of incredulity." Amaziah, the priest of Bethel, was highly vexed at the pronouncements of Amos, who warned of God's coming judgment on Jeroboam and the people of Israel. Amos was no extraordinary prophet. He lacked the sophistication, flamboyance, and eloquence of some high prophets, but he knew that God had called and anointed him to preach judgment to the people of Israel. Amos was not well connected politically. He was not part of the political and religious establishment. He was not part of the in crowd, but simply a "country preacher," a herdsman, a dresser of sycamore trees whom God had anointed to bring a Word to the people from on high. He would therefore would not shirk his prophetic duty. He would not shun this serious and awesome responsibility. He would not be intimidated by the power of the priests and their ruling cohorts. He would stand before them and speak the truth that God had given him, well or ill.

Amaziah, a chief priest at Bethel who administered the golden calf there, was threatened by the words cascading from the mouth of Amos. So concerned was he with the efficacy of Amos' message that he lied to King Jeroboam, saying that Amos had prophesied death against the king. Amaziah knew that this was treason in the highest form and that such insolence would bring certain death to Amos! Amaziah was uncomfortable with the presence of this country herdsman, speaking fire and brimstone and shaking the foundations of the religious/political establishment. Thus the stage was set for a classic confrontation between priest and prophet. By what authority did Amos speak? By what authority did Amaziah command Amos to prophesy elsewhere?

A number of key issues may be derived from this text which set the stage for the clash between priest and prophet between these two cities of action and belief. Both claimed an indisputable authority which emanated from God, but the realms of authority and their attending concerns were at issue here.

First was the conflict between political authority and spiritual authority. Amaziah was concerned about the welfare of King Jeroboam. He was an integral player in the brokerage of power in Israel. The high priest often functioned at the behest of the king, so Amaziah's concern would be to please and appease the king first in all things. He understood that most power was concentrated in the king of Israel. The high priest would not only administer the religious rites of the temple but also would equally function as a political ally, as eyes and ears for any seditious activity in the kingdom. Any perceived or real threat would be immediately reported to the king, so that any potential uprising could be summarily and thoroughly crushed by the king on a moment's notice.

The reality is that all kings, because of the covenant established between God and Israel, would have the best interest of God's kingdom at heart. But Jeroboam was stubborn and self-centered. He veered the people of Israel off their spiritual course by erecting idols in Israel in order to keep people away from the temple. He appointed priests from outside the tribe of Levi and depended more on his own gambits and cunning than on the promises of God. He essentially wanted to usurp the power and authority of God through his political administration but was careless and would not change his evil ways.

As a votary of the king Jeroboam, Amaziah was probably corrupted by the vices and devices of the king's administration. Everyone in Israel knew this, and the priest had essentially lost all moral and spiritual authority.

This is a problem in the church today. Some priests and ministers are more interested in serving the men who occupy the thrones of leadership in the church's hierarchy than the God who commissions such leadership in the first place. The problem is the corruption of power and the power of corruption even within religious institutions. We have repeatedly observed these traits from the early persecutions to the Spanish Inquisition, where priests have blindly followed the higher prelates of the church virtually to personal ruin out of loyalty to their rulers. Amaziah appeared to be a priest who would do anything to preserve his power, even if it meant lying to the prophet.

Amos, on the other hand, was more concerned with serving God than the people of the kingdom of Israel. Amos wanted to do God's will and bidding by exhorting the people back to God and by warning them of the coming scourge. God probably chose someone as plain and naive as Amos to prophesy to the people because Amos had lost respect for temple ministrations. The religious establishment had become corrupted because it was more interested in serving the king rather than spiritually serving God and the people of his kingdom.

Amos understood that the current dilemma of the people of God was due to their tendency to place men above God rather than God above men. The general failings of the covenant were due to the idolatry of hero worship, which had flourished in Israel as a cult reality. Whenever the people of God place men and women and the power and authority of institutions above the will of God, the covenant is broken. This was Israel's problem. It had turned firmly away from the spiritual traditions which gave them success over their enemies.

How could Amaziah tell Amos when and where to prophesy when he had become corrupted by the very men against whom Amos was sent to prophesy? By what authority could Amaziah prevent Amos from preaching God's word? Amaziah had compromised his spiritual and moral authority to a corrupt political establishment and was part of the problem of Israel's demise and not part of the solution to its long-term health and vitality.

Second was the conflict between maintaining order and transforming order. Amaziah did not want Amos to rock the boat. The prophet was an embarrassment to his administration. The people were listening and hearing the words of the prophet, and this was a threat to the status quo. Amaziah wanted to maintain things as they were. He wanted to stay in his comfort zone. His job was to see that discomfort or anxiety did not unsettle the king, and Amos' words were particularly annoying.

Amos wanted to transform the status quo and he would do this at the request of God, who commanded him to speak. Amos would not have business as usual. The sorry state of affairs among the people had reached a new low and the time had come to do something definitive about the problem.

As people of God we must do more than maintain the status quo. We must do more than keep the corrupt and disingenuous in their tranquil state. The prophet comes to upset, to comfort the afflicted and afflict the comfortable, and Amos was willing to do this for the restoration of the souls of God's people.

Nothing is more vexing in our modern society than a corrupt and moribund priesthood, who administrate and caretake a church which is generally disinterested in saving souls, feeding the hungry, housing the homeless, and clothing the naked. They specialize in maintaining things as they are. They never raise a voice of protest, never challenge the existing order, never take risks and leaps of faith on behalf of God's people. They hide out in their temples and sanctuaries, in their plush-carpeted offices and abodes, never hearing or tending to the cries and needs of the depressed and oppressed. They maintain the current corruption by never challenging the establishment to repent or raise a higher standard and make good on its promises to the people.

When the church does not cry out in protest against the evils and corruptions of this world, God truly grieves. As Dietrich Bonhoeffer once observed, "Only he who dares cry out for the Jews dares permit himself to chant in Gregorian." This same truth may be applied wherever there is desolation and oppression among the people. The church must cry out, "Thus saith the Lord." But such is difficult to achieve if the priesthood is corrupted by the political power. We need not only an active priesthood of all believers but equally, in the words of James Luther Adams, a "prophethood of all believers." Numerous churches have lost the respect of the world because of their failures to transform or to speak prophetically to current social and political evils.

Priests have often been ridiculed for wanting to maintain rather than transform the existing order and prophets have been ostracized for wanting to transform that order without a concern for establishing order. But the truth is we need both. We must, in the words of Alfred North Whitehead, "preserve order amid change and change amid order." It does not suffice simply to maintain the church or to maintain its ministry without a concern for a transformation which brings human wholeness and the realization of human potential.

Amos' concern was calling the people back to God and into an awareness and action by effecting long-term positive change which would engender long-term results. He was not concerned with establishing political connections, placating the king, currying favor for his prophetic office and orders, or obtaining a place on the board of directors of the nation. Amos was concerned about doing God's will, and this would require boldness, tenacity, and courage to bring the word of truth to the political powers of his times. The concern is not to maintain the current corruption and apathy, but to transform the hearts, minds, and souls of the nation and to retrieve those time-honored principles which consolidated Israel's power as a nation and made it a formidable adversary.

Just as we can never manage ourselves into the kingdom, we can never simply be content with maintaining things as they are. Amos understood the necessity of transformation. He knew the hazards of maintaining things as they are. He knew that God was fed up with sin, lies, avarice, lust, betrayal, greed, corruption, and the wholesale crimes of influence peddling among the religious establishment. Israel had lost her sanctity and Amos was interested in restoring it in the name of God. The priest wanted to maintain order while the prophet wanted to transform that order.

Third was the conflict between professing the sacrament and living the sacrament. Now we know that the sacraments in Israel's time were not as we know them in the new Covenant tradition. However, "sacrament" here means the acknowledgment and practice of consecrating and making sacred the things of God. The sacrament is the process of sacralizing and making holy the things that are God's. For example, the administration of the rites of temple were a kind of sacrament in Amos' time. The oblation of certain offerings as atonement for sin was sacrament. Any action or activity which invokes the awareness and practice of the sacred or the divine among the people is sacramental.

The priest must do more than profess the sacred or simply be a passive exponent of all things sacred, but the priest must equally live his or her life in the zone of consecration and sanctity. This was a major disparity between Amaziah and Amos. The sacrament of life and living holy had to be more than a thought or belief that one professed. It had to be lived amid the myriad desecrations and profanities of real-life experiences. The Word of God would have to be lived with head and heart, body and soul. One must do more than give mere lip service to the sacred but must live life out within these realms of reality and possibility.

The religious and political establishment had lost their sense of the sacred. They abandoned those precepts, concepts, and beliefs which allowed them to live consecrated lives. That's why God chose an outsider, a most unlikely person to prophesy unto the people.

Living life sacramentally means maintaining the vertical spiritual connection in all things. It means doing God's will and work without regard to outcome. It means doing God's will and work as God has commanded without compunctions, reservations or fear.

Amos knew that Amaziah had lost all moral and spiritual authority as a priest and therefore did not possess the power to deter the prophetic imperative to prophesy unto the nation. The priest was appointed. The prophet was anointed. Only God has the power to affirm or quench the prophet's desire to speak the truth on behalf of God.

We today need to retrieve such moral authority in doing God's will and work as both priest and prophet by standing on and speaking the truth. We must claim our authority and vouchsafe our right to speak that truth whenever and wherever God's Word demands. The offices of priest and prophet need not be diametrically opposed. Those who are called and anointed of God can maintain their temples and still bring a word of hope and transformation for a suffering people. It is only by such conviction, power, compassion, and resolve that the people of God can be won back to God and souls can be saved for the coming time. The authority by which they both think and speak should be an authority that emanates from God and should be preserved without comprise unto the ends of the earth. True spiritual authority issues from God, and those unwilling to uphold that authority are not worthy of service to the people of God! True spiritual authority comes from doing God's will, knowing what is right, and doing what is right. The compromise of spiritual authority often leads to a conflict of authority, and this was the case of Amaziah and Amos! But by holding fast to the things of God, as did Amos, we can restore sanctity and order in spite of the conflicts and challenges we face! Amen!

Lectionary Preaching After Pentecost

The following index will aid the user of this book in matching the correct Sunday with the appropriate text during Pentecost. All texts in this book are from the series for Lesson One, Revised Common Lectionary. (Note that the ELCA division of Lutheranism is now following the Revised Common Lectionary.) The Lutheran and Roman Catholic designations indicate days comparable to Sundays on which Revised Common Lectionary Propers are used.

(Fixed dates do not pertain to Lutheran Lectionary)

Fixed Date Lectionaries *Revised Common (including ELCA)* *and Roman Catholic*	**Lutheran Lectionary** *Lutheran*
The Day of Pentecost	The Day of Pentecost
The Holy Trinity	The Holy Trinity
May 29-June 4 — Proper 4, Ordinary Time 9	Pentecost 2
June 5-11 — Proper 5, Ordinary Time 10	Pentecost 3
June 12-18 — Proper 6, Ordinary Time 11	Pentecost 4
June 19-25 — Proper 7, Ordinary Time 12	Pentecost 5
June 26-July 2 — Proper 8, Ordinary Time 13	Pentecost 6
July 3-9 — Proper 9, Ordinary Time 14	Pentecost 7
July 10-16 — Proper 10, Ordinary Time 15	Pentecost 8
July 17-23 — Proper 11, Ordinary Time 16	Pentecost 9
July 24-30 — Proper 12, Ordinary Time 17	Pentecost 10
July 31-Aug. 6 — Proper 13, Ordinary Time 18	Pentecost 11
Aug. 7-13 — Proper 14, Ordinary Time 19	Pentecost 12
Aug. 14-20 — Proper 15, Ordinary Time 20	Pentecost 13
Aug. 21-27 — Proper 16, Ordinary Time 21	Pentecost 14
Aug. 28-Sept. 3 — Proper 17, Ordinary Time 22	Pentecost 15
Sept. 4-10 — Proper 18, Ordinary Time 23	Pentecost 16
Sept. 11-17 — Proper 19, Ordinary Time 24	Pentecost 17

Sept. 18-24 — Proper 20, Ordinary Time 25	Pentecost 18
Sept. 25-Oct. 1 — Proper 21, Ordinary Time 26	Pentecost 19
Oct. 2-8 — Proper 22, Ordinary Time 27	Pentecost 20
Oct. 9-15 — Proper 23, Ordinary Time 28	Pentecost 21
Oct. 16-22 — Proper 24, Ordinary Time 29	Pentecost 22
Oct. 23-29 — Proper 25, Ordinary Time 30	Pentecost 23
Oct. 30-Nov. 5 — Proper 26, Ordinary Time 31	Pentecost 24
Nov. 6-12 — Proper 27, Ordinary Time 32	Pentecost 25
Nov. 13-19 — Proper 28, Ordinary Time 33	Pentecost 26
	Pentecost 27
Nov. 20-26 — Christ the King	Christ the King

Reformation Day (or last Sunday in October) is October 31 (Revised Common, Lutheran)

All Saints' Day (or first Sunday in November) is November 1 (Revised Common, Lutheran, Roman Catholic)

Books In This Cycle C Series

Gospel Set
Sermons For Advent/Christmas/Epiphany
Deep Joy For A Shallow World
Richard A. Wing

Sermons For Lent/Easter
Taking The Risk Out Of Dying
Lee Griess

Sermons For Pentecost I
The Chain Of Command
Alexander H. Wales

Sermons For Pentecost II
All Stirred Up
Richard W. Patt

Sermons For Pentecost III
Good News Among The Rubble
J. Will Ormond

First Lesson Set
Sermons For Advent/Christmas/Epiphany
Where Is God In All This?
Tony Everett

Sermons For Lent/Easter
Returning To God
Douglas J. Deuel

Sermons For Pentecost I
How Long Will You Limp?
Carlyle Fielding Stewart, III

Sermons For Pentecost II
Lord, Send The Wind
James McLemore

Sermons For Pentecost III
Buying Swamp Land For God
Robert P. Hines, Jr.